The '

B

MW01600386

One man's story about a brotherhood of hang gliding pioneers!

Robert Combs is a pioneer hang glider and light sport powered aircraft pilot who started flying in the early 1970s. During 50 years of flying around the world, he experienced exciting and memorable flying moments. Once he discovered the sport, there was no looking back. It would be the defining passion of his life.

The sport took him to some of the most exotic and spectacular locations on earth as he continued a quest in search of the highest mountains and most beautiful sites to fly.

A highlight of his career was being selected to be the actor, stuntman, and technical advisor for a series of Wrigley's Chewing Gum commercials that were aired around the world.

During his world travels he met and flew with other pilots who are still friends to this day. Robert added some of their insightful and personal stories of memorable flights to this book.

*This book is not intended to be a
complete history of the sport of hang gliding.
It is rather the story of my life as one of the many
pioneer pilots from the late 1960s and 1970s who
were able to experience man's lifelong dream of
flying and soaring the skies like the birds.
It is also the story of the lifelong friendships
that developed among those pioneer pilots who
braved new frontiers as they were given*

The Wings of Men

When I was just a small boy living on Pinkham Creek in the mountains of Montana, I had this recurring dream of running as fast as I could down this steep trail toward our homestead in the meadow below. I would be jumping over rocks and tree roots when I would suddenly fall forward and fly like Superman just above the trail. Our barn in the meadow would suddenly appear and I would soar up and right over the top of it and land on my feet!

I loved this dream, and it kept recurring until I took up hang gliding in my 20s. And then it went away and never returned. I like to think it was because I satisfied my yearning to fly like a bird with "The Wings of Men."

I am so fortunate to have been able to live my childhood dream.

Introduction by Darlene Cecil

We, mere mortals on the ground, could only gaze in awe as we watched the early hang gliding enthusiasts. These pioneers left fears behind to satisfy a deep and somewhat transfixing desire to fly like birds. They climbed steep mountains, bravely walked to the rocky edge of cliffs, hooked into their gliders and ... remarkably ... jumped off with nothing more than sailcloth held together by thin aluminum tubes.

We would all gather, expecting to see spectacular crashes. But somehow, they would sail in the air above us and then gently glide to the ground. OK, some met the ground with a little more force than others. But those who were naturals, were simply mesmerizing as they sailed around in circles and figure eights and then landed lightly with a simple push forward of their control bars.

Robert Combs was one of those natural flyers from the very beginning. When he asked me to edit this book, I said "How interesting can that be?" Well, I was in for a pleasant surprise. This book appeals to hang glider and trike pilots, both new and old, as well as to those armchair thrill seekers among us who long for the freedom and excitement that only pioneers of a sport truly understand.

The book covers 50 years of memorable travel, exciting flying, lifelong friendships, and a total evolution of the sport.

I invite you to sit back, start reading and become a passenger in Robert's remarkable life.

With love to my children:

Christopher Combs, Timothy Combs, and Jessica Lenz,

and to my granddaughter, Madison Gilcrest.

Robert, mother Ellagene, Christopher, Timothy, Jessica and Madison.

~ I would like thank my editor, Darlene Cecil. I could not have published this book without your expertise.

~ Thank you Marius Jovaisa, Unseen Pictures, for the cover and other photos.

~ Thank you Dana Wickenheiser for helping to create a great cover design.

Click on this **QR Code** with your smart phone camera
to be directed to Robert's website featuring
color photos from various chapters.

Website: www.thewingsofmen.com

The Wrigley's commercials and various videos can be
seen on Robert's YouTube channel at:
Robert Combs (The Wings of Men)

Chapters In a Life Well Lived

Otto Lilienthal

Francis Rogalla

Chapter 1
In The Beginning

This is a story about hang gliding and young men and women who were pioneers in the sport. My name is Robert Combs, and I was fortunate enough to be one of those young men.

Otto Lilienthal was the first hang glider pilot. That initial development in flight happened when Otto, known as the "flying man", made and flew the world's first glider in the 1890s in Germany. How amazing it must have been to be the first person to fly like a bird!

Hang gliding was a new sport in the early 1970s and it grew like wildfire in the U.S. and Europe. At one time, there were more than 100 hang glider manufacturers. It was, and is, a sport that allows people to fly and soar like you have wings coming out of your back. It gives you a feeling of freedom like no other. When flying with other dedicated pilots, a very special bond takes place and you become "friends of a feather" for life! Why?? Because only they <u>truly</u> understand what joy this sport causes and why it becomes a lifelong passion.

In 1902, Orville and Wilber Wright built their powerless foot-launched glider and flew it off the sand dunes of Kitty Hawk. Little did they know that by adding power to their glider, that powered airplanes would become the focus of the flying world. Powerless, foot-launched flight would pretty much be placed on "the back burner" other than bungee launched and towed sailplanes.

That is until Francis Rogallo designed his flexible flying wing. In his 2009 Los Angeles Times obituary, it said he was considered the "father of modern hang gliding" for inventing a flexible wing in 1948. He had been an aeronautical engineer researcher for what is now NASA, and they were interested at that time in his design concept to guide spacecraft to a pre-determined location on the sea. But, in the end, they could not work out a proper guidance system for his flexible wing design. Luckily, he remained undeterred.

Francis tirelessly worked on his idea and developed the lightweight wing at his Virginia home with his wife, Gertrude, a former seamstress. They cut the first prototype from their old kitchen curtains and later tested models in makeshift wind tunnels in their basement. By 1951, they had patented a flexible wing with fabric that spread into a fan shape with help from wind pressure.

"Such a flexible wing does not exist in nature," Rogallo told Invention and Technology Magazine in 1998. "Even birds' wings have bones and a rigid shape."

I was lucky enough to meet Francis Rogallo while operating my Water Gliding project in the Outer Banks of North Carolina. John Harris of Kittyhawk Kites was kind enough to introduce me to Francis. I remember thinking, "Wow. I am meeting a man who is a true legend in his own time." It was a moment I will never forget.

Foot-launched gliders didn't come on the scene until the late 1960s when an Australian water skier named John Dickinson designed, built, and flew a man-sized version of the Rogallo-style wing that he towed behind a boat. His kite used aluminum tubing and sailcloth and introduced the A-frame control bar. Before that, the flat kites as they were called used a squared control frame. These kites were also towed by boats. Dickinson discovered that his glider flew on its own after it was accidentally released from the boat tow line.

Shortly thereafter, two young Aussies, Bill Bennett and Bill Moyes, began flying this glider design by also towing behind boats and even cars. These two men also became legends in their own time.

Bill Bennett personally told me a story about his first trip to the United States. He was in New York when he had his glider towed up by boat, released it from the tow line, and flew around the Statue of Liberty. Can you imagine what the people on the ground were thinking as they looked up and saw the man flying like a bird? Upon landing, people rushed up to him, including a police officer who gave him a stern warning, but let him go.

Bennett also went to Lake Havasu, Arizona, and towed up and around the lake and then landed by the famous London Bridge.

Both he and Bill Moyes eventually designed their own hang gliders and became major manufacturers. Bennett manufactured in Los Angeles, CA. Moyes' company started in Sidney, Australia, and it is building world-class hang gliders to this day.

In the late 1960s, some young men in Southern California started making foot-launched kites of their own design and the sport of hang gliding was truly popularized. Bob Wills started Wills Wing Hang Gliders in Southern California and this company grew to be one of the largest, if not the largest manufacturer, of hang gliders in the United States.

Bill Bennett, Robert and Bill Moyes at Sun and Fun Air Show, Lakeland, FL.

Robert in the two-place Blanik, all-aluminum sailplane in Kalispell, MT.

Chapter 2
A Life-Changing Friendship

The first young man I started to fly gliders with during those early days was Tim Schwarzenberg.

I met Tim in 1973 while snow skiing in his hometown of Mount Shasta, CA. I was working as a timber faller and Tim was going to college on the G.I Bill. He had recently returned from a tour in Vietnam while serving in the Army. I also had just returned from a stent in the U.S. Air Force where I learned to fly a small single-engine airplane named the Cessna 150. I had experienced snow skiing at Big Mountain Ski Resort (now known as Whitefish Mountain) in my hometown of Whitefish, MT. However, I must admit, quite a bit of my ski time was spent in the pub. I was an average skier at best. Tim, however, was a top-notch skier who had competed and won the Skimeister trophy in Lake Tahoe. So, my skiing ability greatly improved just trying to keep up with him on the slopes, instead of spending so much time in the pub.

I moved back to Montana the next spring. Tim and I had become good friends and kept in touch by phone. Tim had taken a job mounting bindings at a ski shop in Mount Shasta and he became known as the Ski Butcher.

In the fall of 1974, I took a ski trip to Sunshine Ski Resort in Banff, British Columbia, Canada. While riding the chairlift, I saw a brightly colored kite sail over me with a man hanging beneath! He was seated with skis dangling from his feet and he just came floating by. I was amazed!

In Montana, I had been flying a two-place Blanik all-aluminum sailplane at the Kalispell City Airport. The sailplane had to be towed up by an airplane to get aloft. But here I was on a chairlift, and I just saw a ski-launched glider!! I caught up to the man at the top of the ski hill where he was setting up the contraption for another flight. He had a heavy Austrian accent, and his name was Willie Muller. Willie later became known as Mr. Hang Gliding B.C. Canada.

I'm sure I was driving him totally crazy with all my questions — and all he wanted to do was fly again. He finally said, "if you want to purchase and learn to fly one, go to Invermere, B.C., and look up a glider manufacturer called Eagle Delta". He said, "ask for Barry Howie and tell him Wille sent you." Well, my skiing weekend was over after only one day. I checked out of my room and headed for Invermere!

I met Barry and ended up buying a hang glider and taking a flying lesson from Dean Kupchanko, an instructor at Eagle Delta. We were able to carry the folded gliders, known as Standard Rogallos, on our shoulders while riding the lift to the top of Fairmount Hot Springs Ski Resort. We set up the two gliders, put little orange trick skis on our boots, pointed them and the gliders down the mountain. Dean said, "just follow me and push out or pull in gently on the control bar on my command." That was it, we started skiing down the mountain with a child's swing seat attached to our bottoms. When the glider lifted off the face, I was beyond exhilarated!! It was so incredible!! We were just floating down the mountain, flying above the trees and all the skiers. Dean said we would land at the bottom near the lodge.

Well ... I noticed I was quite a bit higher than Dean when we reached the bottom. At the last moment he yelled out "pull in!" When I did, it seemed like I was just going to hit the lodge a little faster and harder! Just before hitting the lodge, Dean yelled "push out". I did and the glider nosed up into a stall and parachuted down landing on a ski rack full of skis. Somehow, I didn't get a scratch. A friend was on the lodge deck and took a photo of me with my arms fully extended, hanging in the air, eyes and mouth wide open! After that very first hang gliding flight, I was instantly and forever hooked! I am proud to say that my instructor, Dean, later took second place in the first world championships in Kossen, Austria, in 1976.

Well, once I got back home, I called Tim to tell him of my new discovery and that I had purchased a hang glider. He laughed and said, "you won't believe this, but a guy named Jeff Joby showed up at our ski shop today with hang gliders. My boss bought two!". Tim said Jeff simply told us how to set up and fly them. Tim chuckled and said, "My boss agreed to buy them if I would be a test pilot, so I promised I would try it". Tim ended up buying one of the hang gliders from his boss, thus starting a new adventure. He strapped it to the roof of a small U-Hall trailer with his life's belongings inside and towed it behind his MGB-GT sports car. His destination was Montana, so we could learn to fly them together.

Tim and I had been talking about his move to Montana before, but our joint discovery of hang gliding just sealed the deal. That was 1974.

A memorable thing that happened to us that same year when Tim and I were at Moose's Saloon in Kalispell. We were having pizza and beer when in walked Evel Knievel. He strutted into the Saloon with his entourage and made quite a sight being all dressed up in his white leathers with the stars and stripes and his diamond studded cane. Now, remember we were in

Kalispell in the 70s and nobody wore anything but t-shirts and jeans. Evel definitely stood out in the crowd. People parted as he walked toward the bar to ring the brass bell signaling FREE beer for all. The promoters with him started passing out flyers advertising his upcoming Snake River Canyon jump.

The bar was packed, and we were sitting at a long table when Evel came over and sat at our table. I don't remember the conversation that started this, but Evel challenged Tim to an arm wrestling match. Tim was not a big man, but he was very strong and in great shape. When he began to get the best of Evel, Evel jumped up and said, "I don't have to do this ... I'm Evel Knievel"!

Evel then invited us outside to see his 18 wheeler truck with dual trailers. The first was a camper of sorts with a big king-sized bed with a skylight in the roof. The second had several of his custom Harleys and other motorcycles, and of course the truck and trailers were all beautifully painted with his logo. It was quite a striking setup.

Evel's rocket powered jump over the Snake River Canyon in Idaho was nationally televised and there had been an unprecedented amount of press coverage leading up to the event. Unfortunately, it was a failure because he accidentally blew his parachute out when only halfway across the canyon. Instead of completing the jump, he and the rocket floated to the canyon floor. Fans around the globe watched closed-circuit broadcasts in movie theaters, and then ABC's Wide World of Sports aired the event a few weeks later. He luckily landed on the bottom of the canyon still alive.

Years later, I went to Evel's house in Spokane while visiting a fellow hang glider pilot Ed Burris who knew him. I met his young son, Robbie, while there. Evel was born and raised in Butte, MT, where he is buried after passing at only 69 years old. The Guinness Book of World Records shows that Evel sustained a shockingly high number of 433 broken bones by 1975 and his career did not end until five years later. It's no wonder as Evel led a wild and crazy life.

Monument dedicated to Evil Knievel in Twin Falls, Idaho.

Chapter 3

Getting Our Wings

At the time, my good friend Lyle Lucky and I owned a busy little cedar shake roofing mill in Kalispell. It was a great little business and afforded me the time to pursue hang gliding.

Not long after his arrival, Tim and I met Ed Burris and his 16-year old son, Kirk, who also were new hang glider pilots from Helena, MT. We all taught ourselves to foot launch the gliders on smaller hills. But, of course, we were always looking for higher mountains that were a bit more challenging.

In no time, Tim and I found ourselves on the summit of Teakettle Mountain at the entrance to Glacier National Park. It is a 3,000-foot vertical summit from the valley floor. We originally got there on dirt bikes and were inspired by the view. We found some cooling fins off an old radio station and threw them into the wind. We were amazed to see them blow back up and over the top. YES, we decided, this would be a perfect launch site for our hang gliders.

On the following Saturday morning that spring, Tim and I loaded our gear on the roof of his Toyota Land Cruiser and headed to Teakettle. Luckily, we had decided to put a dirt bike on the rear of the Land Cruiser. We were about three-quarters to the top when we came upon a downed tree blocking the road. Our only option was to balance a glider on my shoulder while riding on the back of the motorcycle behind Tim to the top — or nearly to the top. Thankfully, that first hang glider, called the Standard Rogallo, only weighed about 35 pounds, but it was 20 feet long! When we got to the summit the wind was blowing a steady 10-15 miles per hour. The wind was coming straight up the face – but MUCH more wind than we were used to flying on the smaller hills.

But who should go first??? We drew straws and I don't mind admitting I was very relieved when Tim won the right to fly! After all, these lightweight gliders were only made of sailcloth and aluminum tubing! Well, after standing at the launch for what seemed like 30 minutes or more with the glider resting on his shoulders, and me holding the nose, Tim finally said "Well I guess this is as good a day as any to die!" I'm sure the fear on my face was quite evident. I ducked out of the way, and he ran into the wind with the glider. The glider lifted off and flew smoothly off the mountain.

I can still hear his wild YAHOO as he flew away. I stood there transfixed on him as he descended over the edge and then he totally disappeared. My heart was pounding because I knew he had to fly across the wide Flathead River at the bottom before reaching the open field to land. I ran as fast as I could to the motor bike and flew (as a matter of speech) down the steep backside of the mountain. My heart was racing, and I almost crashed several times before I got to the Land Cruiser.

I hurriedly loaded the bike and drove like a mad man back down the mountain and to the landing field. When I got there, Tim was still running around the glider jumping up and down shouting about the amazingly incredible experience, and how well the glider flew!! It really was a "once in a lifetime moment" for Tim. Fortunately, for both of us, there were many more such memorable experiences to come.

We originally had planned to drive back up for my first flight off Teakettle that afternoon. Unfortunately, we didn't have enough daylight left, so I had to wait until the next day for my turn. OK, let's be honest here — I didn't get much sleep that night with the anticipation of the next day's event, but we both knew we had discovered the most amazing opportunity in the world to fly like birds!

We were able to find a driver and our flights the next day together were absolutely phenomenal. I had never before felt such an overwhelming joy mixed with absolute GRIPPING terror! We were flying just like the eagles we had seen soaring there so many times before. We were completely out in the open, feeling the wind on our faces and enjoying the smells of the mountains. For the first time, I truly appreciated the term of "Montana … Big Sky Country." I was able to uniquely experience the wide open panorama of this beautiful place. I remember intently looking at the Flathead River as it flowed down out of Glacier National Park and through Bad Rock Canyon. It was beyond epic! It was the coolest thing I had ever done! I was instantly hooked on free flight!

The gripping fear of that first flight diminished over time as I became more confident in the glider and my ability to fly it. And, of course, landing the glider without crashing into the hard ground was a learning experience as well. We discovered it was important to land into the wind and to flare the wing at just the right moment to land on our feet and NOT our face. Our landing field, which was actually a farmer's field, was flanked on one side by the busy highway leading to Glacier Park. Plus, there were huge power lines coming from the Hungry Horse Dam and power station on the other side. And we can't forget that we had to clear two barbed wire fences on approach to the landing site. There was little or NO room for error.

Thankfully, other people were mesmerized by what we were doing. We always seemed to have a driver volunteer to bring the Land Cruiser back to the landing field for us so we could both fly again. Good thing because it turned into a passion to fly every evening after work and on weekends.

At that time, Ed and Kirk Burris, just like Tim and me, were flying standard Rogallos; Bobby Conat, Don Burks and Jerry Sanderson had Seagull 5s; and David Pearson had one of the first Eipper Quicksilvers. We all started soaring Teakettle together for hours at a time. To say we were hooked on this amazing sport would be an understatement.

Robert preparing to launch on a VERY windy day at Teakettle.

Launching on Teakettle.

In the August 2019 issue of Air & Space Magazine, Paul Glenshaw wrote an excellent article. To me, it is one of the best descriptions of what it is like to fly in a hang glider. The following is an excerpt from that excellent article.

"We first flew in dreams, but the dream of flight has become real," the narrator says. The image on the giant screen is mesmerizing: Above massive volcanic islands reaching up from the ocean floats a tiny triangular form. This is the first shot of the hang gliding scene from To Fly!, *the iconic IMAX film made for the opening of the Smithsonian National Air and Space Museum in 1976. It has been playing for more than 40 years, and for many, it's their first encounter with hang gliding.*

In the scene, pilot Bob Wills hangs below the wing, shifting his body to exert control over the impossibly simple craft. He soars between mountain peaks, then climbs, stalls, dives, and swoops high above the water. When the film was made, hang gliding was emerging from its infancy and about to experience a popularity boom.

Building on a tradition of homemade gliders starting with Otto Lilienthal, Octave Chanute, and the Wright Brothers, flying enthusiasts in the 1960s and '70s fulfilled the dream of accessible, inexpensive, birdlike flight for humans. Hang glider pilot Erika Klein, communications manager for the United States Hang Gliding and Paragliding Association (USHPA), explains why the sport caught on. "If you ever flew a kite and wished you could be flying up there with the kite -- (but) flying free, flying away," she says, "that's basically what it is. It's just a big kite, and you're attached to it, and you can go pretty much wherever you want."

The fundamental design of the hang glider has remained fairly constant since it came together in the 1960s. The pilot lays prone, suspended in a harness at the center of gravity beneath (usually) a swept wing. The wing is made of fabric and metal tubes and reinforced by external bracing and internal spars and ribs called battens. The top half of the pilot's body pokes through a triangular frame -- two downtubes and the control bar. Pulling in on the control bar causes the glider to dive and gain speed. Push out and the glider climbs and loses speed. Shifting the body left turns the glider left; shifting right turns it right. Foot launches are made off hills, dunes, mountains, and cliffs, but gliders are also towed aloft by airplanes, trucks, ATVs, and even scooters.

"You can fly slowly, in control -- the thrill of maneuvering through the sky," says Bruce Weaver, who has taught hang gliding at Kitty Hawk Kites for more than 30 years. "It's something that's hard to describe; once you start doing it, it's something you never want to stop."

Weaver's right -- it is indescribable, but I'll try. In almost every other kind of flight the pilot or passenger is seated, and the apparatus of the flying machine is visible -- you see the fuselage around you, the wing above or below you. But in a hang glider, the wing is mostly out of the field of view. You look out ahead and see nothing but the sky and landscape. You look down and there's nothing between you and the ground but air. You hang from the straps in the harness and your body is free to move. The air is tactile, the wind in your face and ears. The clouds are so close you can actually touch them.

I've launched off training hills, taking off with nothing but my own foot power (and a gravity assist). To run and fly -- even such a simple flight -- is a dream come true. As Dennis Pagen, the leading authority on hang glider safety and training says, "When you dream of flying, do you fly around seated in a chair or are you floating like Superman?"

Flying high — almost

One of many hang glider pilots in the valley this weekend gets set for a descent from the Rollins area Saturday afternoon. About 30 pilots are expected today at Teakettle Mountain near Columbia Falls for the first annual Kalispell Fly-In. Descents should start about noon and there is a concession area at the landing site. Spectators are welcome.
Photo by Darlene Burns

The above newspaper photo and caption was printed in the Daily Interlake in Kalispell, MT, in the mid 1970s. The bearded man to the right is Robert's cousin, Mike Workman.

Notice the photo byline. Darlene, who wrote the story and took the photo, would end up being a significant part of my future. As fate would have it, 40-plus years later, we met again, and we have been together as a couple ever since.

Chapter 4
Flying Makapuu

When snow covered the mountains that fall of 1975, we could no longer navigate the road to the top of Teakettle. We were aching to get in the air again, but how? Around that time, an issue of Hang Gliding Magazine came out featuring a story about hang gliding on the cliffs of Makapuu on the island of Oahu, Hawaii. I just couldn't get my mind off Hawaii and was determined to go experience flying on the ocean cliffs. Ed Burris decided to go as well because it was 30 BELOW zero in Montana. Unfortunately, Tim could not go because he had commitments with his drywalling jobs.

The magazine said we could rent hang gliders from the school in Oahu, so we only had to fill our backpacks with camping gear and our padded swing seats. The article also explained how you could camp free on the state park beach at the base of the ridge flying site.

Ed and I took turns reading the magazine again on the flight to Hawaii. We were amazed that pilots were able to soar in the smooth ocean winds for hours at a time. It emphasized that duration records were being set all the time.

Upon arrival on Oahu, our flight was met by pretty Hawaiian girls in bikinis with stacks of leis around their necks. We each got a lei and a kiss on the cheek with a sweet "Aloha" welcome. It was around 80 degrees with white puffy clouds floating along the green tropical ridge. I could not believe the weather difference in just six hours of jet flight! I knew instantly that this was going to be my new winter home!

We got on the Oahu bus system with our backpacks and asked the bus driver to take us to the beach park where the hang gliders flew. He knew just where we wanted to go -- a place called Waimanalo. When the bus dropped us off at the beach park, we could see hang gliders soaring above on the ocean cliffs. Another camper told us they were landing just around the corner by Sea Life Park. But he warned us not to leave our tents with possessions inside, as they would be gone when we returned. So, we decided to wait until morning to go and find other pilots.

Just before dark, Ed and I were sitting on the beach enjoying the view when suddenly we heard a swish above our heads. We looked up in astonishment to see a hang glider flying just above us. It landed right in front of us in a perfect flare landing. We ran up and quickly introduced ourselves as "visiting hang glider pilots from Montana". He was a young Hawaiian named Kalani who looked only 16 or 17 years old. He quickly folded his glider and another young man arrived in a van to pick him up.

Before they left, Kalani asked if we would like some pakalolo. We didn't know what that was but soon discovered 'paka' meant tobacco or smoke and 'lolo' was crazy Hawaiian slang for marijuana.

We all went into my small tent. The other young man produced some Hawaiian beer, and we lit up the pinner of Maui Wowie. Soon hang gliding tales were flowing. Kalani in his Pigeon English slang told us about the wooden platform built out over the edge of the cliff where the trade winds blew straight up the face, usually at 15 to 30 miles per hour! He said the launch person would hold the nose of the glider from the front flying wires to keep you from blowing back off the box until ready. The launch person, on the command "clear", would then let go and duck down and Kalani said he would leap into the A-frame or control bar with his feet and soar the cliff while standing in the A-frame! Well, I had about enough of this wild tale and exclaimed, "Kalani, I know we are pilots from Montana, but I know you don't jump into your A-frame on launch!!!" Kalani jumped up dramatically and said in his Hawaiian pigeon slang *"you like to beef bra"*, *"you calling me a liar"*, which I understood to mean "you want to fight". I said I didn't want to fight, and he said "everybody ... in the van ... NOW"!

We all clamored into his van, with his glider on top, and headed for launch. It was after dark and I'm thinking I'm about to witness a suicide! We had to unlock a gate to access the road to the top of the cliffs. You had to be a club member to have a key. When we got to the top, Kalani quickly set up his glider. You could see all the lights of humanity along the beach and the trade winds were blowing at least 20 MPH. I was wearing a blue and white Porsche insignia jacket and Kalani asked if he could borrow it for the flight. I gave him the jacket, but I exclaimed that he didn't have to show us at night because we could wait for morning.

The two of them carried the glider out to the ramp at the cliff's edge. Kalani hooked in, steadied himself and yelled *"Clear"*! The nose of the glider quickly flew up, and at the same moment, he jumped into the control A-frame with his feet directly on the base tube. He began to soar above our heads yelling down *"I told you Bra"*! We were amazed ... and remember we were all stoned on Maui Wowie!! And that was my introduction to flying hang gliders at Makapuu, Hawaii!

The next day, Ed and I rented a glider and a two-week vacation for me turned into a month of some of the most fun I'd ever had while flying a hang glider. Ed had obligations back in Montana, so he flew back home. I paid the fee to change my return flight date and stayed two additional weeks. That was back when it only cost $50 to change a flight.

I purchased a homemade Standard Rogallo from Ray Hook. It had an all-white sail with a blue picture of Icarus air-brushed onto the sail with the words, Oahu, Hawaii. I paid $300 for it.

I had run out of money and had not eaten in a couple days when I boarded the flight back to Montana. That's when they used to feed you on their flights and, boy oh boy, was I looking forward to that meal!

Kalani preparing to launch the box at Makapuu in 1975.

My homemade standard Rogallo on Makapuu.

Chapter 5
A Life Changing Decision

When I returned to Montana, I sold my share of the cedar shake mill to my partner Lyle and made plans to return to Hawaii and start a flying school. What starting a flying school really meant was taking people on tandem flights for hire.

I rented a little cottage right on the beach and earned money by taking people on flights in my newly purchased Wills Wing "Raven" tandem hang glider that I flew off the cliffs of Makapuu. I could land my glider on the beach right in front of the cottage at the end of my flying day. It was magical!

The hang gliding flying conditions at Makapuu were some of the best in the world for ridge soaring. The North North/East Pacific trade winds are known for blowing continuously for days and even weeks on end and they blew right up the face of the Makapuu ridge line. These trades were smooth as glass and the ridge soaring was amazing!

The world duration record was originally set there by Bob Wills, the pioneer pilot and hang glider manufacture from Southern California and then by another Wills named Jim Wills who was a jeweler from Honolulu. The record was for 33 hours. It is a record that I believe still stands today.

After that, the record for "distance traveled in a hang glider became the big challenge among pilots.

When the moon was full and the ridge was lit up with a magical green glow, we would attach strobe lights to our gliders to avoid having a mid-air collision while soaring for hours in the lunar light. The white sand beach would light up like a runway when landing.

In those early days, we had car cassette players with battery packs in pouches that we sewed into the belly of our flight harnesses. With great headphones, we could pump the hits of the early 70's into our ears while soaring like birds. From the ground, we looked like twinkling stars in the night sky.

Tandem hang gliding at Makapuu.

The following is a story written by my friend and fellow hang gliding pilot Jim Nurse, who now lives in Washington state.

There were a few nights that were profoundly different. In Hawaii there are a handful of very special nights where the full moon is just rising over the Koolau Mountains, the trade winds are light but steady from the northeast and there are a few scattered clouds drifting along. On such a night, and with a couple quick phone calls, I would be part of a small group of hang glider pilots that would be headed out to Makapuu with our gliders. We had the special "golden" key to the gate that would allow us access up to the top of the ridge above Waimanalo. On those special nights the moon would still be bright and full. So bright you could differentiate colors.

The trade winds would still be steady. The rushing air, cool but not cold. There was always silence as each pilot rigged his glider. Serious business that required total focus. After all the gliders were set up, we gathered together and smoked some of the best pot found in Hawaii from our pals on Maui. It was 1976 after all. I had my battery powered cassette tape deck ready to go. And as I lined up on the launch platform a thousand feet above the shoreline below, I would punch in "Pink Floyd's Dark Side of the Moon", then it was the big tug of the glider harness, and the ground would be left far below.

"The sun is the same in a relative way but you're older, shorter of breath and one day closer to death"
"Far away across the fields the tolling of the iron bell calls the faithful to their knees to hear the soft spoken magic spell."

The glider launch is exhilarating. You become part of the wing in the ridge lift as the ground falls away far below. Things begin to settle after gaining another thousand feet of elevation above takeoff and then the view becomes overwhelming. Looking across the Kaiwi Channel from two thousand feet up the lights of Maunaloa on Molokai glitter and twinkle.

Turning the glider to the west along the ridge the view is stunning and almost magical as all the lights of Honolulu spread out below. I pondered the thought that just a short time ago I was down amongst those lights but now I am drifting in space under a bright Hawaiian moon far, far away. Even now, thinking back, a great quiet comes over me to capture and relive those hours aloft.

A night flight adds up to a long day and eventually it becomes time to turn the glider east once again and head to Makapuu and the landing zone. One by one each glider

29

departs the ridge lift and sails out over the water and breaking waves for a few final turns to set up a landing. Everyone flies down and lands safely. There are few words spoken between us as the gliders are disassembled. The magnitude and intensity of the flight does not need jubilant shouts, high fives and congratulations. Knowing looks between pilots is enough.

Everyone now heads their own way home as the intensity wears off. In a few days we will most likely gather somewhere and share our individual recollections.

When asked about these flights later (or even today) all I can say is that they were really special.

Mahalo Jim, I couldn't have said it better!

Because the flying conditions at Makapuu were so constant, a person could fly almost every day. This ability to fly so frequently produced some of the most-skilled hang glider pilots anywhere.

Among these early pioneer pilots were John Hughs and Steve Leder (who built and flew a hang glider made of bamboo and black neoprene plastic). Steve took me on a tandem flight in his custom made standard Rogallo – seated side-by-side -- from Diamond Head Crater in Waikiki. As we were soaring above the crater, we noticed a pretty girl on the concrete pad where we had launched. We looked down in shock because she had taken off her top and was providing a very memorable topless show. After soaring for about half an hour in the Kona winds (which means the wind was coming from the Big Island of Hawaii), Steve flew back over the crater, and we landed in Kapiolani Park.

Other pilots were Gary Claiborne, Dudley Mead, Michael Vandorn, Rick McCadi, David Goto, (who still flies there today) and Bob Thornburg (who hooked a camera to his wing painted like a butterfly and took a photo while soaring the ridge that became a popular poster across the U.S.). There also was Paul Courtney who started flying hang gliders at the very young age of 14 in California with early pioneer and manufacturer Bob Wills. Paul competed in early competitions and was one of the top hang glider pilots in the country. Paul now lives in his home country of New Zealand and still flies his hang glider.

Others included Timothy Kern, Ray Hook, Ed Cesar, Mike Benson (still flying Makapuu to this day), and Steve Rayfield, (who manufactured Olomana hang gliders that were specifically made for the conditions of Makapuu). He flew with his girlfriend Blyth Coulter, who sewed the best and cleanest sails in the business. There also was Bill Chamberlain (who went on to become a captain for a major airline), Jim Nurse, Randy Eneim, Duff King,

Tom Veer, John Thorp, Dave Neto, Jeff Cotter, Roy Haggard, (who became a world-class designer of hang glider wings for Ultralight Products), Linda Tracey, Barry Gordon, Randy Zimmer, Tommy Namias, Jerry Charlebois, Bill Boyum and David Darling from Maui, just to name a few.

Another fun part of that era was listening to a popular Hawaiian band named Kalapana. They wrote a song called "Naturally" about hang gliding on Makapuu. I remember a constant flow of visiting pilots from all over the world who came to experience the great flying conditions and the warm and sunny beaches!

In 1976, after living and flying with the local ridge pilots on Oahu, I was invited on a flying adventure to the Island of Kauai. It was my introduction to, in my opinion, the most beautiful island in the Hawaiian chain. There were four of us and we all had standard Rogallo gliders of the day, and I was still flying seated. It was going to last a full week. We loaded our gliders and gear in a cargo plane and headed for Kauai. It was a DC3 cargo flight flown by our friend and fellow hang glider pilot Duffy King. We all had backpacks with enough food to last for a week. We took mostly grains as we had been told that the Kalalau Valley had an abundance of avocados, papaya, oranges, and other native Hawaiian fruits. We also brought sleeping bags for nights on the beach. We left Oahu after dark, knowing we would have to set up camp that night and then get up before dawn.

Early the next day, we had to get up to the Kalalau Lookout and carry our gliders out to the 3,000-foot vertical cliffs before daylight. I was told not to slip on the trail as it would be my last. It was pretty scary, but worth the trip up. When the morning light arrived, I saw the Na Pali Coast for the first time. Wow, it was spectacular!! I was astonished at the pristine beauty of the place! There were amazing sheer cliffs cascading steeply down these glowing green spines to the beach and the sparkling blue Pacific Ocean. To this day, I can close my eyes and envision that moment. It is one of the most stunningly beautiful places I have ever seen.

While standing at the top, we could see a large yacht on the ocean, and it had steam pouring off its deck. We learned later that it was a movie crew filming King Kong with Jeff Bridges and Jessica Lang. They made steam on the deck by wetting down dry ice to make the island look mysterious as they filmed through the mist. It was such a memorable scene.

After I launched from the cliff face, I noticed a helicopter flying nearby with a piece of plywood painted to look like a yellow Caterpillar tractor slung beneath it. The helicopter flew close to me, and I was afraid of the turbulence created by the spinning blades, so I circled down for a landing on the beach. Almost immediately, the chopper pilot set the plywood prop down and landed next to it. He jumped out of the chopper and ran up to me saying that he had never seen gliders like ours before. I told him to go to Oahu to find out more. I learned later he showed up at Makapuu and told the pilots there that he was an experienced hang glider pilot and rented a glider from them. Amazingly, without ANY hang glider experience, he flew it from the box launch and landed on the beach. His name was Larry Newman. Larry became a major manufacture of ElectraFlyer hang gliders out of Albuquerque, New Mexico.

Another memorable experience of that trip came about because it was Spring Break. To my astonishment there were a lot of college kids who had hiked the 12 mile Kalalau Trail along the Na Pali coastline to spend spring vacation in paradise. Much to my surprise, it was a nude beach party. My friends hadn't shared that little tidbit with me. I was in the air about to start a final glide to the beach when I looked down and saw a couple of girls sunbathing. I remember thinking those girls look naked. I was concentrating on making a good landing, and not embarrassing myself by landing on my face, so I didn't get a proper look from the air. I was able to make a perfect flared landing. I stood there and was simply awe-stuck by the beauty of the place and the blue Pacific Ocean. I turned just in time to see the two girls bounding my way, or should I say bouncing up to me, completely nude! YES, that was a memorable day of flying! I was caught off guard and didn't know where to look as they were excitedly asking questions and gushing about how cool it was to watch me fly and land. I decided to look down at my hiking boots! After all, this was not a common sight in Montana!

They welcomed us to the party and said follow us, so we did. They took us to an awesome cascading waterfall that fell down the cliff into a shallow pool. Someone had carved out a place in the rock face for a bar of soap. They said "off with your clothes ... EVERYONE goes nude here". I am normally not shy, but this was kind of embarrassing. Okay, REAL embarrassing! But we did undress as the girls stood by giggling.

Well, remember this was morning and in all the excitement of flying someplace new, I forgot to add sunscreen to my backpack. Here, I stood on a beautiful beach with giggling young women who could not help but look at my VERY white Montana butt. Before the day was over, my white butt and my private part were extremely and very painfully sunburnt!

We spent an incredible week in paradise on the beach and in the Kalalau Valley of the Napili. We were picked up a week later by a pre-arranged helicopter and simply tied our folded gliders to the skids for the flight back to civilization. That whole experience was an adventure of a lifetime, and I will never forget that magical week.

In the photo above notice his backpack as he prepares to launch seated.

Preparing to launch from the Napali Cliffs, Kauai, Hawaii, 1976.

Chapter 6
Tragedy at Makapuu

In 1976 there were a lot more pilots showing up to fly hang gliders at Makapuu. And in June of that year, there were five tragic accidents and three pilots killed!

I was in one of those accidents and Ray Hook was involved in another one. Ray was flying the cliffs by the lighthouse when his incident occurred. These cliffs bottomed at the ocean with the waves crashing against them.

Ray didn't have enough lift or altitude to make it back to land on Makapuu Beach. He crashed against the cliffs but was able to hang on and unhook from his glider which allowed the glider to tumble down into the ocean waves. Miraculously, he was able to climb up to safety. Later, Ray said he could see his glider under the water riding the waves.

One of the pilots killed was preforming whip stalls above the launch pad. A whip stall is a type of intentional stall in which a glider goes into a vertical or almost vertical climb, pauses, slips backward momentarily, and drops the nose downward. On the last stall, the glider pitched straight down, tucked, and crashed on the top of the cliff killing the pilot. This was before dive recovery was designed into our gliders.

Another pilot was performing wingovers above the landing area at Sea Life Park. These maneuvers put a lot of G-force on the pilot and his well-worn harness straps tore apart and he fell from his glider and hit the ground among the pilots in the landing area. He was killed instantly. I witnessed this accident, and it was terrible!! I don't remember the third fatality.

My accident happened when I had purchased a new hang gliding harness from a California company. I had sold my existing harness to another pilot so I could not fly until my new one arrived. I decided to go up to the launch and help wire pilots from the box (as we called it). It was a perfect north day which means the wind was blowing at a 90-degree angle and straight against the cliffs. This caused the lift ban to extend way out over the ocean.

Lance Carstens, a fellow pilot from the North Shore, asked me why I wasn't flying on such a perfect day. I explained my new harness hadn't arrived and I had sold my other one. He said, "I have an extra one in my car you can use" and then I wired him off the box.

I immediately ran to his car and found he harness. I looked it over and put it on. It was a perfect fit, as Lance and I were about the same size. I did a hang check with one of the pilots and everything looked good. I was flying a glider called the Sun 3. It was a newer designed glider called a "cut keel".

I got wired off from the box and I was looking forward to my flight because the flying condition were great! There were 20 or more gliders in the air, and everyone was enjoying the smooth perfect air.

At that time there was an aerobatic maneuver, called a flat spin, that was popular with pilots flying the cut keel glider design. A flat spin is when one wing of the glider is stalled, and the other one is still flying which causes the glider to spin or rotate in a circle. The pilot induces the spin by moving his body to one side of the A-frame control bar and pushing out at the same time.

I was flying about 500 feet above the cliff face, just to the right of the launch, when I initiated the flat spin. After several revolutions, I wanted to come out of the spin, so I pulled in on the control bar and tried to move my weight back to the center. However, I was unable to get back to center. It felt like I was caught on my right rear flying wire!

When I looked over my shoulder, I could see my harness foot stirrup which was attached to the harness with a ring and a snap (similar to what is used on a dog's chain). It was hooked to my rear flying wire which held me to that side of the A-frame. I was losing altitude fast and spinning directly toward the rugged cliff face. In a panic, I let go of the control bar, grabbed the wire with my left hand and tried to open the snap with my right hand. This caused my body to slide down the wire toward the tail of my glider. I crashed right on top of the cliff's edge. Thankfully, I did not hit the face of the cliff because I don't think I would be here to tell this story if I had.

Several pilots saw me go in. They landed at Sea Life Park and called the emergency rescue helicopter. I don't remember the impact. In the flying world it is called task saturation or greying out which means you have too much to do without enough time, tools, or resources to do it. It also happens when your mind registers that it is going to be a bad crash.

I was knocked unconscious and was laying in the middle of the crashed glider. The first thing I remember was hearing the helicopter rotor wings spinning near me. I could barely see a medic above me who had his foot in my armpit and his hands around my wrist. Then, he started pulling on my arm. I was only half conscious, so I started kicking at this man who was really hurting my shoulder. I found out later that my shoulder was dislocated, and he was just putting it back in place.

He loaded me into a rescue basket and when the chopper lifted me up, the basket was slightly head down and leaning over to one side. I felt like

I was going to roll right out! Luckily, I was secure, and the helicopter flew to Sea Life Park where they had a place to land.

There was a newspaper photographer there that snapped a photo of the crew lifting me out of the basket and into an ambulance. The photo appeared in the newspaper with the caption, "Montana Bob not flying today!" Since there were three Bobs flying at that time, my friends distinguished me by giving me the nickname of "Montana Bob". The local TV station news team was also there so the crash story appeared on the evening news.

They took me to the hospital, and I learned that I had a dislocated shoulder and concussion, in addition to a sprained elbow, knee and ankle -- all on the right side of my body. I also had several large gashes, all on the right side, from the heavy brush and rocks that I crashed into on impact. But, amazingly, NO broken bones!

The doctor was amazed that I didn't have any breaks after examining my damaged, bloody body.

When I saw the glider later, the control frame had been sandwiched between the ground and the wing, and the upper wire rigging had totally snapped on impact. Luckily, it looked like the glider took most of the impact and this action undoubtedly saved my life.

Our club rented the flying site for $1 per year from the Bishop Estate. After the accidents, they closed the site for one month. That was in June of 1976.

I, obviously, did not fly for quite a while because I was in a wheelchair for a week and then I hobbled along on crutches for a month or so.

This is the Easy Riser that Tim and I built in our garage in 1977. See Chapter 7.

Chapter 7
Back to the Mountains

Once I recovered from the crash, I returned to Montana and knew I simply had to fly again. Tim said it was time to *"get back on the horse"* and fly again.

That first flight was at my favorite home flying site of Teakettle Mountain. I was a bit nervous, but once in the air I felt right at home again. More than ever, I realized how much I loved this wild and crazy sport.

That summer, I was once again joined by Tim and our other flying friends Ed, Kirk, Jerry, Bobby Conat and David. We flew off Teakettle Mountain every day in the late spring and summer afternoons when it didn't get dark until 10 p.m.

About that time, Tim and I together bought a fixed wing hang glider kit called the Easy Riser. It was being made by Larry Mauro in California. It came in a large box with complete instructions on how to build it. It was a bi-wing design. You had to build the four wings, even making ribs for the wings. The ribs were made with formed foam and pine cap strips. It had an aluminum framework and provided instructions on how to build the jig to set the framework in to get the correct sweep and dihedral in the wing design. There were aluminum sheets that we cut to make the joints in the frame -- all put together with hundreds of pop rivets! Once we got the wings built, we covered them with a special cloth that had to be brushed on with a dope liquid that we dried with a hair dryer. The dope made the cloth shrink to a beautiful tight and quite durable wing surface.

We built the Easy Riser in our garage it truly was a thing of beauty. Its performance was way ahead of anything else flying in those years. The two bi-wings broke apart at the nose and folded down on each other for transport on top of our Land Cruisers. Once you got the glider assembled at launch, you had to wedge your body between parallel tubes that formed a cage-like enclosure. It had twist grips that, when rolled, operated the drag rudders out and in between the wing tips.

When in flying position, the upper wing was slightly above your head and the lower was about waist high to leave your legs out for the run into the wind and off the hill. Once airborne, hanging from just your armpits, you kicked your legs up and rested your feet on the front bar that we wrapped in foam and covered with a leather sheath. There also was one at your back for comfort. You were sort of wedged in the control frame. Pitch was done by sliding your weight back and forth between the parallel bars and roll was achieved by the twist grips that controlled the drag rudders.

We decided to test fly it at our flying site adjacent to Flathead Lake. We had a beautiful 2,000 foot vertical hill with a smooth rolling grass launch. It also had a smooth wind blowing up the hill off the flat surface of the lake. The bonus was a nice landing field down in front. Perfect!

There were still patches of snow on the ground that spring day when we finally navigated to the launch site. I remember it was chilly, but we were dressed for it. Plus, we had overwhelming excitement and anticipation for that first Easy Riser flight. Adrenaline alone kept us warm.

We decided Tim would fly it first as he led us on most all our new flying adventures. It seemed as if he had feathers growing out of his back and head. He just had a natural talent. We decided the best place to learn how to fly it was in the air with lots of room and nothing to run into.

The wind on launch was a steady 10 mph. Tim made his dash and the glider nose floated up immediately. He quickly kicked his feet up on the front bar, the nose of the glider came down and he soared smoothly off the hill in a noticeable climb. I jumped up and down and yelled "all right"! It was a beautiful sight! After making a perfect landing at the bottom, we broke the glider down, loaded it and headed back up the mountain for my turn! We assembled the glider while Tim gave me quick flying instructions. I was ready!

The wind was still blowing a steady 10 right up the face, so I leveled the wings and noticed immediately how much lift those wings produced. I had to keep forward in the cage to keep the nose down. I started my run and the nose suddenly pitched up ... I kicked my feet up for the front bar ... and missed! "OH SHIT," I exclaimed quite loudly! The nose rose up into a stall and I sort of did a barrel roll to the right and up on the nose of the glider. I could not believe that neither the glider or I had any damage after a close examination. So, naturally, I decided to try again! Well, it was almost an exact repeat of my first attempt! So, I made the decision to quit for the day while both the glider and I were still in one piece! I had Tim as a partner in this glider and I had no desire to wreck it on our first day out.

Tim and I eventually each bought Canadian hang gliders called Eagle Delta and became dealers in Montana. I had one named The Eagle, so I had it painted like an eagle with its talons outstretched. It was very colorful and memorable. The Canadian artist who painted it was well known and his work was quite popular in Canada. During the early 1970s, hang glider designs were changing almost yearly due to innovation and development.

Soon thereafter, Tim and I each bought a new design of hang glider called the Highster. It was one of the first double-surface hang gliders and was made by Mike Giles, a manufacture in San Francisco. Our friend Ron Ridenour was the dealer in Montana and all three of us owned one.

Tim, Ron and I traveled to Invermere, B.C., with our new Highster gliders to fly with our Canadian pilot friends off Mount Swansea. There were always a lot of American pilots who came to fly there. Eventually, it turned into a large summer competition called the CanAm Challenge. There were as many as 60 or more pilots who came from all over the U.S., Canada and Europe for the fun and comradery.

When the snow started to blow, I headed back to Hawaii for the winter flying season, but I was back to Montana the next summer. That was 1978.

It was a summer filled with more high mountain flying adventures. On top of our list was to return to the competition in Invermere. It was growing rapidly in popularity and was attended by my friend and top Hawaiian pilot Ed Cesar. Tim and I slept in a teepee on the shore of a lake owned by a fellow Canadian pilot in Invermere. Ron, Tim, and I purchased a helicopter flight with our gliders to the top of the mountain range above Fairmont Hot Springs Golf Course for the final day of flying.

Tim and I hit the hay early that night as we wanted to be in good shape for the next day of flying. Sometime in the night, I was awakened by Tim screaming crazily. I fumbled for my flashlight and fully expected to see him in the clutches of a bear. He was sitting up in his sleeping bag with eyes wide and the look of horror on his face. I said, "what the hell, you scared the crap out of me!" "I just dreamt I fell out of my glider!," he stammered. We talked for a few minutes until Tim was calm and able to go back to sleep.

The next morning at breakfast, Tim told all the pilots at our table about his crazy dream. The pilots said, "wow that's heavy" and "that's crazy man!"

After breakfast, we were ferried by helicopter to the mountaintop above Fairmont. We unloaded and set up our gliders at the launch site. We were hoping for thermals to start popping so we could work our way above the launch for more altitude. The first couple of pilots to fly didn't find any lift so it was pretty much a sled ride to right above the golf course where they would land.

Then it was my turn. I carried the glider out to the launch where the launch director watched me hook into my hang straps. He then held the nose of the glider so I could lay down in my harness and he could do a "hang check" which meant he checked to be sure all my harness lines were straight and not tangled and that I was at the proper distance above the control bar base tube. He cleared me to launch and just then I heard Leroy Grannis say, "hit the release button". Grannis, who was a staff photographer for Hang Gliding Magazine, had hooked his camera to the cross bar leading edge junction of my glider. I touched the electric release button for the motor winder on his camera and nothing happened. I was familiar with this system and knew he hadn't turned on the motor winder out at the camera. He wasn't allowed to approach the glider after I had been cleared to launch, so I sat the glider down, unhooked from my hang straps, went out to the camera, and turned on the motor winder.

I hurried back to the glider A-frame, hit the button, and heard the camera fire. "Great, we are a go", I thought. Just then I heard the first thermal of the day start blowing up the face of the mountain. This meant I could potentially catch it and circle in the rising air up and above the launch. I picked up the glider, steadied it, made sure my wings were level and then made a strong run into the thermal updraft. As the control bar base tube touched my face, I suddenly realized ... I had NOT hooked back into the glider! I pushed the glider away and dropped about 15 feet into the rocks below, badly twisting my ankle. The glider rose in the thermal, made a slow left turn and then crashed downwind into the side of the mountain next to the launch. Tim, who had been watching, climbed down to me. I was devastated with the shame of what I had just done -- at an international competition no less! My pride was shattered. I had forgotten to hook back into the glider!

They cut my boot off to reveal an ankle that was most likely broken as it was swollen and severely bruised. I was lucky to be alive, but I felt such remorse in making such a stupid mistake. Somehow, I had not broken the ankle, but had a very bad sprain which the doctor said could be worse than a break. And mine was. Well, that was the end of my flying for that day. Tim and Ron flew while the helicopter took me to the hospital.

On the drive back to Montana, I fell asleep with my casted foot resting on a pillow on the dash of Tim' red Porsche. When I awoke and looked around, I realized we weren't on the road home. I questioned Tim and he said, "well, in all the excitement, you forgot it's your birthday so I'm taking you for a birthday supper". We went to a restaurant owned by a fellow pilot in the small town of Fernie, B.C.

Tim was very reflective during supper and said, "if I ever forget to hook into my glider on launch, I'll climb up into the control bar and hook in." He said at some point every pilot will forget to hook in. At that time a surprising number of pilots were listed in the Hang Gliding magazine accident reports and many of those accidents happened because pilots had forgotten to hook into their gliders on launch – just as I had done.

Tim used the restaurant phone to call his sister in Mount Shasta to see if his parents were on their way to Montana. They were driving up to see us and she confirmed that they were on their way. We got home at midnight and sacked out. There is nothing like pain medicines and a long drive to make you sleep like a baby.

Early the next morning, we woke up to loud knocking on our door. It was our friend and fellow pilot Ron Ridenhour. He said, "it is blowing out of the north so Desert Mountain is flyable"! Ron worked for the railroad and lived on Lake Five near the base of Desert Mountain in West Glacier, so he saw the wind conditions firsthand. Tim cooked up huckleberry pancakes for us and asked me if I would bring his folks to the landing area at Desert when they arrived. Obviously, I wasn't in any shape to fly, so I said, "sure I will Tim", and they were off.

I fell back asleep after taking the pain prescription and was awakened by the phone ringing. It was the owner and writer of the Hungry Horse Newspaper, Mel Ruder. In the past, he had done a couple of news stories on our hang gliding adventures so he knew us. He had even won a Pulitzer Prize for Distinguished General Local Reporting, making him the first journalist in the state to be so honored. He told me there had been a hang gliding accident out on Desert Mountain. He said I should go to the Kalispell hospital as the helicopter rescue team would be flying in the injured pilot.

I could not drive with the cumbersome cast, so I had to hitchhike into town. Luckily, a kind farmer picked me up in his truck. Once at the hospital, I went to the helicopter rescue station and heard one of the nurses talking on the radio with a nurse on the chopper. The helicopter nurse said they couldn't find the injured pilot. I asked them if they knew the identity of the injured pilot. They didn't, know.

I called home and spoke with Tim's mother right after their arrival. I told her there had been an accident, but we did not know if Tim was involved.

They immediately drove to the hospital in Kalispell to get updates. We all anxiously waited for the helicopter to arrive, but no news came. After a couple hours and no updates, Tim's dad said, "let's drive out to the flying site". We were on the road to the back of Desert Mountain's launch site when we met Cal Jorgensen, a local college professor of photography, who was driving down in Ron's truck.

Cal confirmed that the downed pilot was Tim. He told us that Ron flew first and then Tim was hooked into his glider preparing to launch when he said, "hey Tim, you forgot to put on your helmet." The professor later said Tim had commented that he had a lot on his mind with his parents due there and all. Tim unhooked from his glider and put on his helmet. Tragically, Tim forgot to hook back in before launching. The launch site is extremely steep, and he was instantly hundreds, if not a thousand feet, above the mountain face. He didn't have the same opportunity as I did to let go and drop to the ground because he was way too high. So, unfortunately, Tim hung helplessly onto the base tube.

In hearing the story, I remembered what Tim had said just two days before -- "if that ever happened to me, I would climb into the control bar and hook in." Cal said it looked like that is what he was trying to do. The glider rocked side to side as he attempted to pull himself up into the A-frame. Unfortunately, by hanging from the base tube, it caused the glider to fly very fast. He said Tim worked his way to one side of the A-frame because he probably was trying to put the glider in a downward spiral to the mountainside. He simply could not hold on and the glider flung him off!

Cal watched him plummet several thousand feet into the thick forest below. Then he lined up rocks at the top on the flat surface to create a noticeable arrow pointing approximately to where he saw Tim disappear into the trees.

Tim's parents and I stayed up on the mountaintop that night as it got dark, but the chopper team had to give up the search and leave. The next morning, a search and rescue team showed up along with my brother, Gary, and a couple other glider pilots' friends, Craig and Carl Ambrose from Missoula who had heard about the accident on the news. The mountain was steep with thick, heavy buck brush and had trees growing on its side which made the search for Tim extremely difficult. The second day after the accident came and went, so we spent another night at the launch site. That night I slept in the back of a truck owned by a pilot friend, Craig Ambrose. At one point during the night, I stood on the launch and started yelling down to Tim, "Don't worry Tim, we will find you." At that moment, I choked up and collapsed. I knew it would be a miracle to find him alive.

On the third day, most of the Search and Rescue team had to leave. Tim's dad said, "let's go to the glider and make a human chain stretched out with as many men as we have left." He recommended that the last man on the chain mark the trees with ribbon as they worked their way around the glider. On the third revolution around the glider, Tim's dad and my brother, Gary, were at the end of the chain when they came upon Tim's body.

My brother said he tried to keep Tim's dad from looking at his son's lifeless body, but his father said he had to know. Gary said Tim had part of a tree branch still tightly clutched in his hand. He said there was a deep gash in his other hand, but no blood, which indicated to them that he was killed

44

instantly and did not suffer. The gash on his hand was probably from the corner bolt of the A-frame when he was violently flung off the glider.

Tim and I had learned to fly hang gliders together. He had been my best friend and we had been roommates for several years. He was an excellent pilot and the first one to try, and excel, at all the skills of this sport we loved so much. The amazing thing is that he had dreamt he fell out of his glider just a couple of days before it actually happened! And, he had told the pilots sitting at the breakfast table of the dream. One of those pilots was Ed Cesar from Hawaii.

Tim died on Aug. 2, 1978. He was only 28 years old. Tim's parents and his friends took the chairlift to the top of Big Mountain Ski Resort where we each said our goodbyes to him. Tim's Dad, a minister back in Mount Shasta, read from the book "The Profit." I can't remember all I said in my goodbye as I was virtually overcome by grief.

We also had Dave Sewart, a sailplane pilot, drop Tim's ashes over his beloved Teakettle Mountain where he had been the first to fly. We stood in a circle in the landing area (around his red Porsche) and held hands as we listened to a song playing on his stereo. Tim loved the song "Wings of a Bird" about flying by Elvin Bishop. Ed Cesar from Hawaii watched in amazement with us as an eagle appeared just as the white puff of his ashes showed in the sky.

Robert Combs and Tim Schwarzenberg two days before Tim died.

EAGLE USA

TIM SCHWARZENBERG   BOB COMBS
406-755-0361

A while later, Ed Cesar made a film titled "UP" about hang gliding. In the film he shows the pilot fall from his glider and suddenly an eagle appears next to another. As a feather floats down from the sky, you realize it's all in a dream. In 1984, Ed won an Oscar for this short adventure film.

(Above) Ed Cesar getting ready to launch. (Below) Early Teakettle flyers.

Robert, in a cast after his accident, with Ron Ridenour on Desert Mountain.

A short time after this tragic accident that took my friend Tim's life, and my accident in Canada, I came up with a solution that I felt could save lives in our sport.

Both accidents were caused by a "failure to hook in" to the glider, so I began formulizing a solution that all glider pilots could use before takeoff.

I used a stainless steel tang with a bungee attached to a red ribbon with the words "HOOK IN" with a ring at the end. The tang was fitted on the underside of the nose plate of the glider so that the ribbon hung down in front of the pilot's face. The only way to get rid of the ribbon was to stretch it back along the undersurface of the sail and hook the ring at the end of the ribbon into the pilot's D-Ring when hooking into the hang straps.

I know the idea was a bit complicated for non-hang glider pilots to understand, but experienced pilots would understand. Very few pilots used this as most couldn't imagine how they could make the unthinkable mistake of not hooking themselves into their glider before launching.

However, most long time hang glider pilots know of this happening or at least heard of it happening to someone. During hang gliding's popularity boom years of the 70's and 80's Hang Gliding magazine included a section in their monthly issue titled "Accident Reports". There was a surprising number of reported accidents that were caused by "failure to hook in."

48

I still find it hard to believe that I did this, and that the same mistake took my best friend's life. Tim Schwarzenberg was the most skilled pilot in our group of flyers. He was also a very safety conscious pilot.

A lot of these accidents happened after the pilot hooked into his glider, then unhooked for something, and then forgot to hook back in. When preparing for a launch there are a lot of things going on that the pilot has to get exactly right for a successful flight. For instance, I had hooked in and then unhooked to turn on the camera's motor winder. I think the action of hooking in the first time satisfied that part of the launch sequence in my mind. I then right away had to level the wings and make a strong run into the air of the rising thermal. Tim had hooked in, then was told he forgot to put on his helmet, so he unhooked. It was a very similar scenario to my accident.

Hand thrown reserve parachutes were becoming a part of every pilot's gear around this time. If Tim had one, it may have saved his life as they are commonly mounted on the chest area of the pilot's harness with the bridal line attached to the harness D-Ring. I purchased one from Bennett Hang Gliders in L.A. shortly thereafter, and from that point on I always flew with one.

There also was a tandem hang gliding incident in Canada recently that gained national attention. The tandem pilot hooked into the glider but failed to hook in his tandem passenger. So, after a successful launch, the passenger hung onto his tandem pilot for what I think was a 2,000 foot glide to the landing field where he let go as the glider was skimming the ground to land.

I don't know all the particulars of this incident. I have taken 100s of tandem flights in my hang gliding career. A lot of times there were people standing around while I was setting up my glider preparing for a tandem flight. Many times, I had to ask people politely to *"please ask me that in the landing area as I need to concentrate on what I'm doing here," "thank you".*

49

Brian Johnson flying his Seagull 5 (above).

Landing area at Mount Sentinel in Missoula in the early '70s (below).
I remember fondly those early days of flight with friends.

Chapter 8
Pilot Tells Story of Missoula Pioneers

While flying hang gliders in the early '70s from Mount Sentinel in Missoula, MT., I met brothers, Bruce and Dale Stoverud. The following is a piece written by Dale.

My brother, Bruce Stoverud, was born in 1949 in Missoula, MT., and died flying his hang glider in Hellgate Canyon on June 19, 1981 -- just five days short of his 33rd birthday. He was a true pioneer of the sport and lifestyle of hang gliding

Around 1973 or 74, he became interested in the new sport of hang gliding and started a typical "garage" business as a dealer in Missoula for Delta Wing Kits & Gliders, owned by Bill Bennett in Los Angeles. He also started teaching others from Stone Mountain in Missoula, me included.

He joined with Jay Raser and called their business The Hanger. Many of us started flying in the mid '70s, graduating with the state-of-the-art hang glider science due to commitments of early dealers and certified instructors.

In 1979, he became certified in single engine aircraft (Cessnas, etc.) and was looking at a future in powered aircraft. His last log entry was June 15, 1981.

Bruce was an early member of the USHGA, and obtained "Observer" status in April 1981, just months before his accident. Over the years, he also became interested in powered ultralights (using powered Quicksilvers) and started a side business called Ultralite Flying Service in Missoula, which stopped when he died.

As a true pioneer of the sport and lifestyle of hang gliding, Bruce also worked with Delta Wing and Ultralite products over the winters in California. He would test fly new designs and promoted the state of the art.

He was always a cautious, responsible flyer. When his accident occurred, he was blown leeside into Hellgate Canyon in a summer squall. He lost control as his glider was winged over and died on impact in his UP Mosquito. It was witnessed by many people on the interstate nearby.

Bruce Stoverud

His death changed the perspective of those family and friends closely involved in the sport. I had small children at home, and the final realization was that it had been a wonderful chapter, and one to be remembered and celebrated as an incredible time in our lives.

Dale Stoverud flying into Aber Day Kegger, 1975.

Chapter 9
Shave a Mustache – NO Problem!

I went back to Hawaii in 1979, but it took a while before I had the heart to fly again after losing my best friend. I knew Tim wouldn't want me to give up the one thing that we both loved so much, but it took time to want to fly again.

It was around this time that I met Phil Sallee on Oahu. He was flying a powered ultralight aircraft called the American Aerolights Eagle. It was built by Larry Newman of Electra Flyer hang gliders in Albuquerque, New Mexico. I believe it was the first commercially available ultralight. It had a small two-stroke engine with a canard wing out in front. It was controlled by drag rudders at the tips of the wings which had wires attached to the swing seat. So, it basically flew in the same way as a hang glider by shifting your weight forward and back for pitch and side to side for turning and roll.

American Aerolights Eagle at dusk.

I bought one and Phill and I enjoyed flying them on the North Shore of Oahu where he had a hanger of sorts at Dillingham airfield. If you go to the
I-Max theater production at the Grand Canyon, you can still see a film depicting an Eagle ultralight flying through the canyon.

That winter, the advertising agency Needham Harper & Steers contacted our flying club on Oahu. They were going to film a television commercial for Wrigley's Chewing Gum that featured hang gliding. There were around 40 or so pilots flying at Makapuu at the time. The ad company rep said if any of the pilots would like a chance to fly in the commercial, they should show up for what's known in the film business as a "cattle call." The agency was in Los Angeles, and they had already interviewed quite a few pilots in California.

I don't know how many of us showed up for the interview, but I do remember wearing my best Hawaiian shirt, shorts, and slippers, also called flip flops. They were the only shoes most of us owned. They said, "don't call us, we'll call you if you have the look we want." Well, about a week later, I got a call from the agency. The person asked if I was willing to shave my mustache if they chose me? I said "NO problem. Those things grow back." He said chewing gum and facial hair just didn't go together. He said, "shave it off and we will come back to Hawaii to do a second interview." I had been wearing a mustache since I was old enough to grow one. I was 31 and after living in Hawaii for so many years, my face was very tan. When I shaved off the mustache, my upper lip was gleaming white and looked huge. I thought "oh no, this will never do"!

I was rooming with Bill Chamberlain, my good friend and fellow hang glider pilot, and his girlfriend. His girlfriend said just put on some sunscreen and go lay on the beach. This seemed like a good idea as the agency wasn't due to show up for another week. Well, I never was very good at just lying on the beach doing nothing, so I ended up body surfing. Of course, the water washed off ALL the sunscreen! When I returned home my lip was no longer bright white – it was now bright red, badly sunburnt and swollen. I thought for sure that I had just ruined any chance of getting the part. After a week, the swelling had gone down and Bill's girlfriend put a little makeup on my lip so I could go to the interview

The agency had rented a room at the Royal Hawaiian Hotel on Waikiki Beach. They had me sit on a tall stool with big bright lights shining on me. They walked around shooting video of me while simultaneously asking all kinds of questions about what it was like to fly a hang glider. Of course, I was passionate about this sport and finally relaxed while telling them about being able to fly like a bird.

After at least an hour of this, I got the same "Don't call us, we will call you". Fortunately, after only a couple of days, they called and said the Wrigley's Company wanted to use me in the commercial. Of course, I was playing it all real cool and relaxed like this was a call I got every day. Internally, I was screaming – ALL RIGHT!

They had already purchased two new solid red hang gliders called The Laser from Bennett Hang Gliders in Los Angeles and we would be using those during filming. They said they would be back with a film crew in two days along with the gliders, harnesses, and wardrobe.

They sent me a photo of Duffy King, who they had also interviewed, and said we could use him as an extra pilot during the launch sequence. They felt we could shoot two launches -- one after the other -- to save time. Duffy agreed and they used one of his launches in the final 30-second commercial.

We went to the Makapuu launch (also called the Box) to set up and filmed for most of the day. The director Roger Brown had lots of Wrigley's Spearmint gum packs with him. I had to peal the paper off the stick of gum, put it my mouth and chew while looking excited about the upcoming flight. After many takes, all that sweet juice was making my stomach grumble and churn. It was getting harder to show pure enjoyment on my face to tie to the script saying ... "for clean fresh taste that goes a long, long way, there's only one Wrigley's Spearmint Gum!"

I had to join The Screen Actors Guild as it was a union project, so I could receive residuals from airing the commercial. It would be a national which meant it would show on all the major networks like CBS, ABC, NBC and so on.

At the time Needham Harper and Steers was one of largest advertising agency in the nation, handling many huge and prestigious accounts. The amount of money I would receive was calculated by the Guild to be determined twofold – because I was the stunt person flying the glider and that they used my face. The only thing that would have garnered me a higher residual rate was if I was a recognizable face, like a known actor, or if I had a speaking part.

It only took about a month for the commercial to air and it turned out to be a hit. The agency rep said Wrigley's Company reported a 10 percent increase in gum sales. They sent a large box of letters to my post office box in Waimanalo, Hawaii. It was full of fan mail they had received from people throughout the United States. I originally answered all the mail. Most of the letters were from young men who wanted to learn to fly hang gliders, but some were from admiring young women. Surprisingly, the fan mail soon became more than I could handle. But, also in the post office box, were all those residual checks determined by the frequency of the ads on various networks. Well, that wasn't too hard to take!

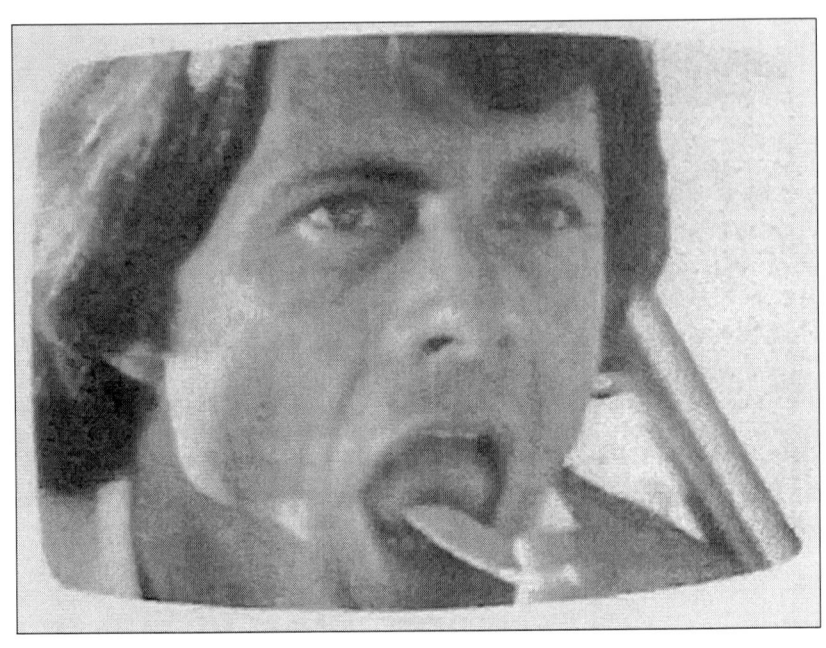

Robert clean shaven for the first Wrigley's commercial.
Below, Robert opening the pack of Wrigley's Gum.

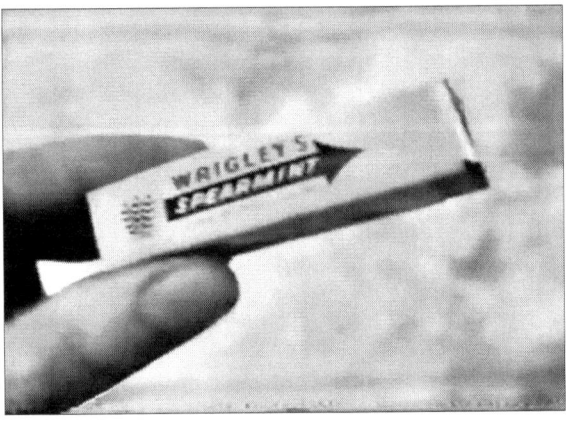

After the TV commercials aired, fellow flyers started calling
me Mr. Wrigley!

Chapter 10
Two More Commercials and New Heights!

After six months or so, I got a call from the ad agency saying the Wrigley's Company wanted to talk to me about shooting more commercials since the first one was such a big hit. The next one would be a mountain scene to compliment the first one shot in a tropical setting. They wanted the new commercials to be aired internationally because Wrigley's sold gum all over the world.

The director, Roger Brown, called and asked me where I would recommend shooting a scenic mountain commercial. I told him about Glacier National Park, in my home state of Montana, and said I thought it would be ideal. He said he would set it up and get back to me. They had to get permission from the National Park Service for me to fly in the park as well as to land a helicopter carrying me and my folded glider up on the mountain peak.

I told Roger I had actually flown my hang glider in the park once before ... illegally. I had flown from close to the top of "Going to the Sun" Road near Logan Pass. I landed on a river gravel bar at the bottom next to the road. Tim Schwarzenberg was at the landing site, and we hurriedly packed and loaded the glider on his Land Cruiser. As you would expect, just as we were headed down the road, a Ranger car raced by us with his lights flashing. They didn't realize it was the glider on our roof top because the sport was so new.

Roger was able to get permission from the Park Service and we all showed up at the Outlaw Inn in Kalispell. The Outlaw was the nicest and largest hotel in Kalispell. We had a film crew that included Roger and his assistant, a makeup person, a wardrobe person, a cameraman, myself (the talent as I was called) and others. A couple guys in the film crew had driven a big truck full of filming equipment from L.A. We hired a local helicopter company from West Glacier to transport us, with the hang glider folded and strapped to the skids, during the filming.

Surprisingly, there was another film crew staying at the Outlaw at the exact same time and they were filming Heaven's Gate. I met the Director Michael Cimino and actors Jeff Bridges, Kris Kristofferson, and Christopher Walken.

After spending a little off time with Christopher Walken, we set up a double date with two girls we had met at the bar in The Outlaw Inn. We took them to Whitefish for a night of dancing. Christopher was a fun guy to party with. There were more than 40 actors in the movie, and I got to meet a lot of them because we were there for nearly a month.

The Outlaw Inn was the most popular night club for dancing in Kalispell and they had a live band playing every night. And, as you can imagine, there was a lot of parting going on with these famous actors in town.

It is unfortunate that Heaven's Gate turned out to be the biggest flop in movie history and supposedly put the movie studio, United Artists, out of business. Cimino had won an Oscar the year before for "The Deer Hunter" which also starred Walken. The Heaven's Gate film crew stayed at the Outlaw for more than six months and had a reported production cost of more than $44 million. It was 240 minutes in length and took a year to edit.

OK, back to the Wrigley's commercial. It was November and, unfortunately, Glacier Park was in low cloud cover. We got up day after day and took the helicopter up to the 9,000-foot-plus mountaintop above Logan Pass only to find the summit shrouded in clouds. To keep busy during the down time, the studio had rented a new 1980 Chevy 4X4 Blazer from the local dealership so I could put a glider rack on it and fly hang gliders with my buddies from Kalispell. Those pilots included Brian Johnson, Gary VanAken, Kirk and Ed Burris, Greg Brau, Keith Volkman and Cory Izett. We flew from lower launches along the Swan Mountain Range that weren't clouded in like the park. With Thanksgiving only a couple days away, Roger called the filming off and we all flew home to be with our families for the holiday.

Once back home in Hawaii, Roger called me again and asked what other options were available for a mountain scene. I said, "How about Austria?". I knew they had held a world hang gliding competition there a few years before and the area was perfect for flying. He said, "set it all up and let's go"! I got hold of a hang gliding shop near Innsbrook and arranged for us to film there. About two days before we were to board flights to Austria, Roger called and said "change of plans, we are going to New Zealand! "You are going to fly from Mount Cook"! I said, "OK let's go"!

But in the back of my mind, I'm thinking WHERE? WHAT mountain? As soon as I hung up, I researched Mount Cook and discovered it was on the South Island of New Zealand. It was the tallest mountain in the South Pacific at 12,500 feet above sea level! It looked like Mount Everest to me!

The photos showed the mountain totally covered with ice and snow with glaciers and huge crevasses. I immediately said out loud, "Oh boy, I hope I haven't bitten off more than I can chew!" Pun intended. Up to this point, the highest mountains I had flown were the 8,000 foot peaks of the Swan Mountain Range near Glacier National Park in Montana.

I knew it was too late to "chicken out" as we were to leave for New Zealand in a few days. I was already halfway there since I was in Hawaii. I met the whole film crew and Roger at the airport and off we went. They had the two red Bennett gliders, a blue flight harness, and all the rest of our flying gear and packed everything in the belly of the airliner. I asked Roger what about my helmet as I was used to wearing a safety helmet when I flew. He said, "we are selling chewing gum, not hang gliding safety". I said, "All righty then"!

We flew to Auckland first. Roger rented a helicopter, and they mounted a huge Gyro (with a chair sitting on top of it) for the cameraman to sit on outside of the sliding door. Roger hired a Pilatus turbo prop to carry the rest of our crew of nine and headed for Mount Cook. As we approached the mountain, I saw the ice covered summit towering (and I mean TOWERING) above us. Mount Cook was sticking up and out of the clouds with snow nearly covering the entire mountain. It looked so unbelievably majestic and awe-inspiring because it was standing alone high above everything in the wide open blue sky.

I simply could not believe they wanted me to fly off that ... and survive!

Let me repeat my thoughts. I simply could NOT believe they wanted me to fly off that and SURVIVE!

We landed at the airport near the mountain base in the little village of Mount Cook. The studio had rented the entire Hermitage Inn, along with a full staff, just for us as the Inn was normally closed for the season.

We also hired a Hughes 500D helicopter and pilot owner Bill Smith at a minimum of four hours a day for two weeks to keep him on the job. Gavin Wills, who had a climbing shop in the Hermitage Inn, joined us as my personal guide. They flew a wardrobe gal and me to Christchurch, the largest city on the South Island, to pick out a wardrobe of women's tights, long underwear, blue Levi's, polo shirt, yellow ski jacket and hiking boots with cleats.

Back at the Hermitage, we got up at the crack of dawn to be at the airport by 6 a.m. each day. The goal was to be ready to film the moment conditions allowed. The summit of Cook was in clouds and winds were reported at 40 mph. This went on for nearly a month and I was afraid we were never going to get this commercial made.

Gavin, Bill, and I flew in the Hughes all over the South Isle while waiting for the mountain to clear. One day, we flew to this amazing geothermal area in the hills and went skinny-dipping in the hot pools. We went fishing for trout in mountain streams where no man had probably fished before. We brought the trout we caught back to the chef at The Hermitage to cook for us. They were great!

New Zealand was just spectacular; a wonder to behold.

I spent evenings after dinner in the Hermitage Bar with the helicopter pilots to go over our flight plans and safety precautions. I told them about Bob Wills, a hang glider pilot, who was killed when he got caught in the wingtip vortices (or rotor) of the filming helicopter while shooting a TV commercial for Jeep in California. So, we were prepared to keep it safe.

Finally, after spending almost a month waiting for the winds to die down and the mountain to clear of cloud cover, we woke up to clear blue skies and zero wind. Roger immediately started excitedly shouting out directions to us. We flew the two choppers up and landed on the 9,800 foot Tasman Glacier (New Zealand's largest glacier). We spread blue tarps out on the flat ice surface of the glacier so I could judge my distance above the glacier when coming in for a landing. Then the Hughes dropped Gavin and me off on the small summit. We had ice crampons on our boots so we wouldn't slide off the steep mountain face. The camera chopper, with the two gliders strapped to the skids, hovered above us. I chose the glider with the larger sail area as there was no wind and the air was thin at that altitude. We estimated the temperature to be around 15 BELOW zero.

Gavin and I hurriedly assembled the all-red Bennett Lazer. We had to jockey the glider side to side to safely put in the sail batons. We each had two-way radios. I also had a mike cord running down inside my jacket arm sleeve with a push-to-talk button on the mike so I could communicate with Roger down on the glacier.

Once we had the glider set up, I had the base tube D-ringed to a steak driven into the ice. Gavin drove another ice steak into the ice at the rear, 90-degree edge of the summit. He threaded his climbing rope through the D-ring and repelled off the near 90-degree edge of the ice cap down the back side of the mountain. He got to a place where the Hughes chopper could pick him up without hitting the rotor blades on the side of the mountain. They plucked him off the mountain side and suddenly I felt very, very much alone on that mountain.

Roger kept telling me they were preparing things for the cameraman sitting on the big white round gyro outside the chopper. I was freezing as I was not allowed to wear gloves so the shot would match the "load shot" as they called the part where I put the gum in my mouth. I had slid rubber sleeves on both ends of the base tube so my hands wouldn't freeze while switching during launch and flight.

As I stood there, I noticed a cloud buildup on the lower mountains around Cook. I radioed Roger and told him I was going to launch in 15 so they better get the chopper up in position if they wanted to get the shot. I knew I would never survive the night on the mountain if it clouded in. I noticed a very light variable tailwind of about 5 mph blowing for about 4 or 5 minutes and then it switched to coming straight up the steep face.

I heard and could see the camera chopper approaching. When the light tail wind stopped and I knew the head wind was coming, I unhooked the base tube from the D ring and ice steak. With my heart pounding in my ears, I hooked into the hang straps, lifted the glider, and felt the tug on my harness straps. I heard Roger yell over the radio "anytime, we are in position".

I steadied the wings and plunged down the smooth, steep mountain face. At first the glider seemed to just drop in the thin air, but then it lifted and flew away! I remember thinking I could hear the most beautiful music in my ears. The flight was the most spectacular I had ever experienced! Bright blue sky and gleaming snow-covered mountains surrounded me. The air was remarkably smooth as glass. And, almost best of all, I pulled off a perfect landing on the Tasman Glacier after a 2,700 foot glide.

The chopper landed nearby, and Roger jumped out and came running over, gave me a big hug and a slap on the back. "We got it", he yelled! We folded up the glider and tied it to the chopper skids. Roger got on the radio and told the other chopper to meet us at Mitre Peak on The Milford Sound while we still had good filming weather.

It was a beautiful flight down to the Sound. We landed on Mitre Peak, the highest rock peak at 5,522 feet above the sound, and quickly set up the glider. The cameraman got into position and this launch was a breeze compared to Cook. I launched above some clouds and had a beautiful and amazing flight down to a small airstrip at the inland end of the Sound. I flew close by a beautiful waterfall just before landing on the airstrip.

When I touched down, a swarm of tiny gnats immediately flew into my eyes and nose. I unhooked and ran away from the swarm. When the chopper came, the wind from the rotors thankfully cleared out the annoying swarm. We packed up the glider and flew back to the top of Mitre Peak where we all slapped hands, celebrating a day of great filming.

Above is my guide Gavin Wills.

Film Crew at the Milford Sound, South Island New Zealand.

Preparing to launch the Bennett Laser above the Milford Sound.

I jumped in the Hughes 500, the pilot lifted off flew out over the sound and did a full loop! I didn't even know a helicopter could do a loop! We flew back to the small airport and headed to dinner at the Hermitage. After dinner, Roger announced he was going to show the rushes (raw footage of the day's filming). He invited everyone, including the hotel staff, to watch the amazing footage. It got a standing ovation from the crew and hotel staff!

The next day Gavin took me on a flight in his two-place sailplane that I'll never forget. His wife towed us up to the top of Mount Cook in their souped up Piper Cub. We released from tow and Gavin flew down the mountain beginning at the head waters of a river. At times, the wings tips were barely off the rock cliffs and just above the river as we flew at a dizzying speed.

When we reached the bottom, he flew under the highway bridge then turned downwind toward the airport. I was thinking he is going to land downwind! But he flew straight down the runway at max speed, pulled up into a 180-wingover and made a perfect landing back on the airstrip ... into the wind! Wow! That was the most amazing flight!

That evening, Gavin invited me to join he and his wife for wine and dinner. They had an amazing rustic older home that he inherited from his father, and it had an incredible wine cellar. His father had been a vintner in days gone by. Gavin dusted off a vintage bottle of fine wine made by his father for us to celebrate and enjoy. That was best wine I had ever tasted ... even to this day!

The next day, we flew back to Auckland on the North Island. Roger and I then boarded a commercial flight to Sidney, Australia. Roger had arranged for us to do the "load shots" as he called them, in a film studio. The "load shots" were important parts of the filming where I would unwrap a stick of Wrigley's Spearmint and insert it in my mouth. I had to do this repeatedly because the closeup image had to show the specific package that was sold in each country where the commercial would be aired. I had to do a lot of takes unwrapping the different ones, sticking the gum in my mouth and looking like I was about to jump off a mountain. And yes, each time I did it, I got all those sweet juices and once again I got a bit sick to my stomach. Somehow, I managed to look like it was the best ever for Roger.

I also had to dress in my outfit and flight harness, stand on a mound of salt that looked like ice and snow for the "load shot" off Cook. I also had to stand on a pile of rocks to match the ones on the Milford Sound. They had large silver and gold colored shields that reflected warm or cool lighting to match the lighting as it had been on the mountains.

While in the studio, there was another shoot happening at the same time. It featured this gorgeous girl who was just in her nickers (the down under word for panties) and a cutoff t-shirt with the lower portion of her breasts showing. There also was an assistant, smoothing any wrinkles on her nickers, and a rather large cameraman with sweat all over his face shooting a very close, closeup of her nickers.

It turned out she was the Australian Playboy Magazine Playmate of the Year. So, naturally, I hung around watching until they were finished. I got very brave, introduced myself, and after a brief chat I asked her out for dinner at her favorite restaurant in Sidney. I told her I had arrived that very day and didn't know my way around the city. To my surprise, she accepted, and we had a great meal at a very nice restaurant with a view of Sidney Harbor. We then had a fun night of dancing in the night clubs of Kings Cross, the hot spot of Sydney.

Below: Robert (center) at Milford Sound with agency guys.

Below: Chopper with gliders tied to skids.

Chapter 11
Towing Gliders Off the Beach

I visited Bill Moyes at the Moyes Hang Glider manufacturing site while in Sydney. I ordered two new custom gliders -- an all-red Moyes Mega (their newest high performance glider) and a Moyes Maxi Mark 2 tandem glider, all red as well.

Bill invited me to stay with him and his wife, Molly, in their high-rise on Bondi Beach. I met Steve, Bill's son, who was a hang gliding world champion. They were getting ready to go to Perth in Western Australia for boat towing of hang gliders off the beach. Bill asked me to join them while my gliders were being built and I accepted.

Instead of flying to Perth with them I opted to take the train for a four day trip across the outback. Well, that turned out to be a "once only" trip as the outback is a huge desert and the scenery doesn't change hour after hour except for passing through small Aboriginal villages where I saw men in loin cloths holding spears in their hands. They seemed to be the color of the red earth on which they stood barefooted. It was like stepping back in time, way back!

Perth was a beautiful seaside town. It's neighbor, Fremantle, is where they were having the Americas' Cup Sailboat races. That was a hoot. Bill and Steve were towing gliders off the beach with a boat. The boat had a static line going from it to a small coil of line on the beach in front of a hang glider and pilot. The line then hooked to a V-bridal and stainless steel base tube with a release. There was another one up at the CG or Center OF Gravity of the glider. There were two release handles, like brake handles on a bicycle, on each end of the base tube. The pilot stood on the beach with glider resting on his shoulders and the keel or tail of the glider was dug into the sand with the nose pointing up. The upper V-tow line was resting on the pilot's shoulder. When ready, the pilot would kick some sand in the air signaling Bill to hit it.

The pilot would hold the glider tight to the ground and as the coils of line straightened, he was jerked off the beach and headed skyward. At just the right angle, the pilot released the upper tow line at CG which allowed the glider to be towed by the base tube up over the boat for maximum height. He would then release the second line at the center of the base tube and go for a free flight back to the beach. The goal then was to land on the bull's eye drawn on the sand. This was a competition and Steve Moyes won landing directly on the center of the bull's eye every time.

Then it was my turn to try it. Bill was driving the boat and watching for my signal. I kicked the sand in the air to show I was ready. I watched as the tow line grew taught and I was suddenly jerked into the air. Unfortunately, the upper V bridal line was caught under the edge of my helmet. When it snapped tight, it lifted me and the glider in a sharp left turn and stalled. Thankfully, Bill did not release the tow line from the boat which would have resulted in a crash back on the beach! Instead, he slowed the boat so the glider and me fell slowly into the shallow water. Bill said, "lets' do it again".

I decided to Velcro the upper V-bridle line to the top of my helmet to prevent a second dunking and got a good tow high over the boat with a clean release and glide back to the beach.

This early introduction to boat towing a hang glider would prove to be very useful to me as I would later design and build a system called "WaterGlide."

This was my first towing experience, and it would later lead to a lot of aerotowing (towing behind a tow plane) as well as boat towing a hang glider. I was thankful for Bill's experience that provided a good first towing flight. For a week, I was able to do lots of boat towing as well as exploring the Western most area of Australia. A memorable part was seeing plenty of "big red" and smaller grey kangaroos. I was amazed to see them bounce along with their long and powerful legs and tails.

I woke up one morning and decided it was time to see more of the world. Bali, a province in Indonesia, was only a short flight from Perth so I decided to go. I was able to get a special package that included a flight to Bali and a week's stay in a cabana right on the beach. What an experience. It had one of the most beautiful beaches and amazingly blue waters that I had ever seen. The cabanas were very basic with no phones or TVs, but the front door opened right onto the most picturesque beach.

It was a great week and then it was back to Sidney.

The red Moyes Mega performance glider was finished and the Moyes Boys "as they were known" took me to test fly it at their premiere flying site at Bald Hill, Stanwell Park.

It is a beautiful seaside launch area with a grass covered rounded hill that allowed for top landings. It is on the escarpment of cliffs that make up the Royal Gorge National Park. After launch, in smooth winds off the ocean, you could turn left and soar for several miles along beautiful cliffs that rose above the sea.

I enjoyed the flight and decided it was time to land. Great idea, but there was absolutely NO easy place to land. I had to be sure the wind conditions were strong enough to keep me afloat. To the right of launch was the quaint seaside village of Stanwell Park. There was a nice beach that bordered a large green grass field. It made a perfect place to land into the smooth winds off the sea. You then could carry your glider back to the grass field for tear down.

After landing and pack up, you and your Mates could stroll over to the small park side cafe for the best Aussi cheeseburger imaginable. Yes, it is one of the nicest flying sites anywhere in the world!

It was now 1980 and I needed to get back to Hawaii to arrange my planned extended world travel!

I did, however, return to Sydney in 2000 to work for a year as a tandem pilot for a wonderful Australian family man, Chris Boyce. He was a hang gliding business owner and extraordinary hang glider pilot.

It was an amazing year. While there, I borrowed a fellow hang gliding pilot's VW Westfalia camper van and took it to several flying sites. I traveled up the Gold Coast to the ever-so-beautiful Great Barrier Reef and the Whitsunday Islands. It was a road and flying trip that I will never forget.

World Champion Steve Moyes boat tows off the beach at Perth, Western Australia.

Chapter 12
Exploring Europe in a Camper

After returning to Oahu, I purchased a new Volkswagen Westphalia camper van on the overseas delivery plan. This plan allowed you to pay for the vehicle at the U.S. dealership and then take delivery at the Westphalia manufacturing plant in Borgholzhausen, Germany.

I ordered the van with an attachable tent and special windsurfing rack that would carry my hang gliders. I then purchased an Around-the-World airline ticket from Pan American that allowed customers to stop off in any country for as long as they wanted.

The ticket allowed you to take flights to countries on either side of your flight direction. These were the Good Old Days when airlines allowed you to take a hang glider as sporting equipment in regular baggage.

I packed my flight harness, with hand deployed parachute, helmet, instruments, in backpack style bag. I packed the new Moyes Mega in the bright orange cardboard tube it came in. It had to be rather comical to see me standing at the end of the baggage claim conveyer, ready to catch the glider as it came whizzing out of the compartment.

I had always dreamed of exotic travels. My original hope of seeing the world was when I joined the U.S. Air Force right after graduating high school in 1966. Instead of exotic destinations, I was stationed at McConnell Air Force Base in Wichita, Kansas, for my entire tour of duty. It was right in the middle of flat land USA. That was a big disappointment, and I couldn't wait to finish my four-year commitment.

So, the Pan American ticket was my chance! I planned to travel to countries that offered the best hang gliding from the most beautiful mountain sites.

The first country I visited was Brazil. I wanted to fly around the arms of the Christo in Rio de Janeiro. Upon arriving and going through customs, the airport customs authorities confiscated my glider. Hmmmm. NOT a good start.

They told me the only way to get it back was when I was on a flight OUT of Brazil. It turned out that a flight attendant, who was also a hang glider pilot from Hawaii, was bringing in hang gliders and selling them without paying the required duty. There were no hang glider manufacturers in Brazil at that time.

One of the pilots there told me the best way to get my glider back was to hire a customs agent. I did this at a cost of $500 and rented a glider to fly in the meantime. At least I still had my flight harness and vario.

I stayed at the round Continental Hotel on Pepino Beach where the hang gliders were landing.

I was approached by a tall blond man who asked me if I spoke English (most everyone spoke Portuguese). I replied it's the only language I speak. He was from Czechoslovakia and his name was Michael Cepria. He said some Brazilian pilots told him I was a flight instructor and he wanted to learn to fly hang gliders.

Michael said he would trade a room in his home for flying lessons. His home was on the mountainside leading to the hang gliding launch called Crocane. Well, the home was beautifully set in the jungle with awesome views of the sea and Pepino Beach. I immediately said, "you have a deal".

I told him about my glider being stuck in customs and that the customs agent had done nothing. He recommended I purchase a flight to Punta del Este, Uruguay, a country bordering Brazil. He said that on my return flight, I should have a $100 dollar bill in the palm of my hand for the customs agent and he would waive any holds on the glider. He said that if I had known the system's inner workings before entering Rio, the glider would not have been delayed in customs. "You just have to know how the system works."

Once we got the glider into Uruguay, the plan was to hire a taxi, strap the glider to the roof and drive to the border of Brazil. Once there, he said I should have another $100 bill for the border agent, and we would sail through.

"Don't worry I will be your guide," he said. Well, we executed the plan, and it worked just like he said. The taxi we hired was a Mercedes and we strapped the glider in its cardboard tube to the roof and drove to the first city in Brazil that had flights to Rio. But this time we entered Rio on the local side of the airport, not the international side. No customs agent. Michael parked his car, a station wagon with a roof rack, at the front and we both carried the glider through the airport. Wouldn't you know that we saw the customs agent who originally confiscated my glider. Fortunately, there was nothing he could do! We hurried out to Michael's car, quickly put the glider on the roof rack and I sat out the passenger door window to hold the glider on the roof as we sped away. I was just hoping that I did not end up in a Brazilian jail!

I taught Michael to fly the Moyes Mega and then sold it to him for a very good deal. He turned out to be an excellent pilot. I stayed in Rio for seven months altogether. A highlight of the stay was working with an American named Rich (can't remember his last name now) to put on the first Brazilian National Hang Gliding Championships. I got to fly around the Christo Statue overlooking Sugarloaf Mountain and the beautiful Ipanema and Copacabana beaches.

I stayed for the famous Rio Carnival celebration which is considered the biggest carnival in the world with thousands of people on the streets each day. That was truly another amazing and memorable experience. We also watched the Samba parade which is a tribute to Brazil's heritage, culture, and history.

After Rio, I flew to Hong Kong. There was no hang gliding there and I didn't have a glider anyway. I purchased a stereo for the camper van and sent it to Westphalia in Germany to be installed.

I also visited Thailand and took a boat tour to see the site from the movie, "The Bridge on the River Kwai." I truly loved the Thai food and the meal on the boat was exceptional.

I then flew to New Delhi, India, and traveled by train to Agra to see the Taj Mahal. My next stop was Kashmir in Northern India, followed by a trip to Kathmandu, Nepal. All together I spent 17 months away from the U.S. on my World Tour with PanAm. This was all made possible by the filming of the three Wrigley's commercials and the residual income I earned for my part. I will always be thankful and feel so fortunate to have been able to see the world, all thanks to Wrigley's Chewing Gum.

My next stop was Germany as I was anxious to see my new VW Camper. That camper became my home while touring the flying sites of Europe and the United Kingdom.

After picking up the camper, I drove to Seeg, Germany, to see the Neuschwanstein Castle completed in 1886 by Bavarian King Ludwig II. The castle is built on a rugged hill that is part of the Alps. It is tucked along the edge of the Bavarian Alps just south of Munich and is considered the crown jewel of Europe's fairytale castles. And, yes, it is also near the Tegelberg hang gliding site.

Robert's Volkswagen Westphalia camper van was perfect for touring Europe.

The flying site uses a tram that takes pilots and their gliders to the top which is 5,200 feet above the valley floor. There are two launch ramps with plenty of set up space and it was the best hang gliding site in the German Alps.

I had heard of a glider manufacturing company close by named Firebird, so I drove to their factory. I met the owners, Fritz & Ian, who were building a new glider design called the Firebird Topless. What made it different was that it had no upper rigging and used struts instead of side wires. It was the first one I had ever seen. They loaned me a demo and we went to Tegelberg for a test fly. It was a bit stiffer in handling than I was used to, but it had a very impressive glide. I could experience the various flying sites of Europe with this glider. They sold me two Firebirds at dealer cost, and they fit perfectly in my windsurfer racks on the camper.

Picking up gliders at the Firebird Factory in Germany.

I called Duffy King in Hawaii and invited him to come over to Europe and fly with me. I told him I even had a new glider that he could fly. I picked him up at the airport in Munich a few days later and we were off on another hang gliding adventure. There was plenty of room in the camper for both of us as the camper also had a convenient side tent. We traveled all around Germany, Switzerland, Italy, and Austria flying the incredibly beautiful sites in the Alps.

While in Innsbrook, Austria, we looked up our friend Martha Zec from Hawaii. She was of Austrian heritage ad showed us all around the country, including the Blue Danube River where the girls wore one-piece bathing suits -- just the bottom piece! Duffy smiled mischievously and said, "Austria is one of the most beautiful places I've ever seen." I agreed! Shortly thereafter, he returned to Hawaii.

Duffy was a pilot for DHL Cargo. He had the great job of flying a DC 3 that carried cargo all around the Island chain. We used to throw our hang gliders and ourselves on top of the cargo at night when he was headed to Maui. Once there, we would rent a car, strap on our gliders, and go to David Darling's place in up-country Kula. We would camp in tents in his yard and then head to the top of the Haleakala Crater in the early morning for a flight. David was the hang gliding guru in Maui.

We would fly from the 10,000-foot summit, soar the shear line before the clouds socked in the top and land on Makenna Beach at the bottom. What an amazing experience it was! We had to fly very early in the morning to avoid the developing clouds. It was unusual to climb above the 10,000-foot launch, but Duffy, David Darling and Bob Allmon were part of the illustrious few pilots to have accomplished this!

I flew with Duffy one other, and last time, at Gold Hill near Telluride, Colorado. The launch is at 12,200 feet. We flew with specially designed oxygen tanks as it was not unusual to climb to altitudes of 15-16,000 feet above sea level. The views of the mountains from that height are nothing short of spectacular!

On our flight day the wind was coming from behind the normal launch, out of the canyon. At those altitudes the air is thin, and pilots said that a successful launch required a strong run to get the glider airborne. Duffy was just ahead of me, and I watched him come close to blowing his launch because he seemed to just amble off the mountain. Duffy was used to flying from the box at Makapuu, Hawaii, his home site, where you simply pushed off into a usually strong wind that required no run at all.

Later that evening while having beers in a Telluride pub, I said "that was close today, Duff, you need to do a strong launch run in the thin air of these high Colorado mountains."

Duff King was one of my closest friends and a very good pilot. But shortly after this trip, he stalled his glider while launching off the cliffs of Molokai, Hawaii, and was killed when he crashed back into the cliffside on launch. He will always be remembered by many of us, his close flying friends of Makapuu, as a great guy who is missed so very much.

Gold Hill launch, 12,200 feet, as seen from the air, Telluride.

The following is an account of hang gliding on the 10,000 foot Haleakala Crater sent to me by my fellow pilot and friend David Darling of Maui, Hawaii. I did not change any of the account and have published it as he has written the story.

A DAY (BUT NOT A DATE) TO REMEMBER ALWAYS

Having lost my logbooks and all photos of my hang gliding adventures in the Maui Wild Fires of 08-08-2023, the date is lost to me forever, and not being able to ask the other two pilots that shared the day with me as Robert (BAD BOB) Allman, and Duff (DUFFY SKY KING) King have both crashed and died. Bob, on the East facing sea cliffs of West MAUI, and Duffy on MOLOKAI at the tallest sea cliffs on earth. The 10,000 foot Haleakala volcano, the largest dormant, now upgraded to inactive, volcano on the earth, does create thermals, but due to a normal low inversion at the 4 to 6,000 ft. elevation getting above launch is not an ordinary occurrence.

This day had a different feel to it, and Duffy, being an airline pilot seemed extra excited to get a chance to launch off the summit with Bob and I. Light and variable winds at the summit had us wondering which side would provide a nice cycle of updrafts for us to launch in the thin air. Lots of waiting around after set up but finally the winds we wanted started to cycle in. Bob was first to launch, I went next and Duffy always one to use others in the air for hints of where to go went last. Not much action on the spine of the mountain leading down to Kanahau peak, which was a known thermal producer at the 7,600 ft. level, a nice bump in the rift zone, before it tapered down to sea level and had vegetation on the low slopes. Little bumps along the way got us excited and we took turns turning in the small pockets of lift. A rare cloud seemed to be forming ABOVE the crater itself, somewhat rare and possible indication that the strange feel to the air signaled a day with no low inversion!!! The bumps got better and better and at the last barren peak that juts above the spine we hooked some good solid lift, allowing all three of us to work back up the spine back towards launch. That had happened before allowing us to get over the launch point and enjoy the spectacular views looking down into the crater itself. Most all of it bare cinders and cones jutting above the crater floor to heights of 12 to 1,500 feet. The crater itself is MASSIVE, all of Manhattan Island could fit inside its confines, but there are only three cabins for hikers, a ranger cabin and a very rustic hunter's cabin, connected by trails and empty space.

All three of us were on the same page and arrived back over the launch point within minutes of each other, and once out over the crater itself, IT HAPPENED, the ENTIRE crater lifted off in a thermal release that was so huge that no matter where you were there was 500 to 800 ft. per minute lift, nice and smooth! New territory but all three of us had thermal experience and stayed with it watching the crater shrink below us as we climbed. The cloud we had seen starting to form on our way back up the spine was forming a beautiful flat bottom cumulus at about 12,800 to 13,000 ft. base was all to easy to accomplish due to the smooth nature of the best thermal I had ever experienced until then, so we all just kept going up into the cloud, topping out at 14,500, a full 5000 ft. above the launch point at 9,500 ft. above sea level. Air quite thin up there, oxygen recommended above 12,500 but I felt acclimated since my training hill was at 4,500 and I would spend two or three days a week at the upper launches.

Duffy spent many an hour at his airline pilot position and Bob was just winging it. He was not prepared for the cold, so to keep some warmth going he would tuck one hand under his arm pit and fly with one hand to try and hold out. Frost bite eventually started to get his attention, so he left first out to the central valley and warm beaches below. Duff and I were gloved up, I had liners as well and always dressed for the coldest possible conditions at altitude. Something finally told me time to leave and at 14,500 most distance records could easily be broken that day. Bob had left so far before me I lost sight of him so I was on my own heading over to the WEST MAUI mountains, that top out at 5,800 ft. Being able to see the wind patterns at sea level on the water I sensed a maybe chance to cross over the central valley well above any airline traffic going to Kahului airport and maybe still have enough to get over to the S.W. side of West Maui and maybe get all the way to Lahaina!!! I set some goals and landmarks on the other mountains and kept feeling good about my chances to get to the other peaks and cross over safely, not knowing that the SKY KING had me in his sights most of the way, he had borrowed my 180 Comet and I was on my old faithful160 which had always done me right, so Duffy had actually used me as a guide and merely followed me from above. Once over the peaks of West Maui I milked it as far as I could getting to the Olowalu surf break, short of my goal of Lahaina but a new distance record FOR SURE! And with a pay phone at the general store, I knew I could get in touch of the pick up after break down. Duffy made it to Puamana just on the outskirts of Lahaina, but after breaking down the glider he flagged down a passing car so he could make the pickup call from Lahaina town!!! He finally had to admit he actually landed in Puamana, but a new distance record was set twice in the same day. He got me on that one and had shared his excitement MANY a time as to how HIGH we did get over Haleakala Crater!!!

Duffy had shared this awesome flying experience when he came to fly with me in Europe.

The 10,000 foot Haleakala Crater on Maui created an interesting weather pattern called the before mentioned wind shear. It was caused when the trade winds collided with the mountain, split and blew around each side of the crater. When the winds met on the opposite side it caused what is known as a wind shear line. One side of the crater is wet from rains and the other is very dry. When the two winds meet, the hotter dry air is forced up and over the damp cool air causing a sheer line and sheer cloud. The sheer cloud forms like a mountain ridge. This also causes a visible dividing line on the ground of the mountain side. The damp air side green with foliage. The other side dry and brown.

We would launch our hang gliders early in the morning from 9,500 close to the summit before the clouds socked it in. We then flew our gliders down to around the 3,500/4,500 foot level where the sheer cloud developed and then soar in the lift along its face. The sheer cloud extended out over the ocean, sometimes as much as 6 mile's out to the small island of Kahoolawe depending on the wind velocity.

One day when David Darling our guide from Kula Maui, Jeff Cotter a fellow pilot from Oahu and I were soaring this sheer cloud out over the sea. I decided I didn't want to fly any further out off the shoreline, I flew out in front of the sheer cloud circled down and headed for Mckenna beach to land. There were some local fishermen who had rod holders stuck in the sand along the shore with their poles with line out in the sea. I made sure to give them plenty of clearance on my landing approach.

As soon as I landed, I unhooked from my glider and looked up for DD and Jeff. I suddenly saw a parachute come floating out the bottom of the sheer cloud. Then Jeff who was flying a new glider design called the Fledge came out of the cloud in a steep dive. The glider nose snapped up and Jeff was flying radically all over the sky. When he came into land, he clipped all four of the fishing poles and sort of crashed onto the sand. I ran up to him and cried out "are you alright"! Jeff wore glasses and they were gone. He had wire rash all over his face and arms. He had the look of terror on his face. He shouted, "I'll never fly a hang glider again!" "I'm lucky to be alive!"

After Jeff had calmed down a bit, while sitting on the sand he told DD and I that he got sucked into the sheer cloud and the turbulence was so violent that he could not keep hold of his control bar and was being thrashed around inside his A frame. He threw his emergency parachute but instead of going out behind the glider it went out front and the bridal line was sheared by the front flying wires. He said he thought he was a goner.

This makes quite a statement for the strength of that glider. Jeff was flying again a week or so later at Makapuu on Oahu.

Another interesting story about hang gliding in Maui was when I was contacted by a film company from France. They wanted me to help make a commercial for the largest bank of France on Maui.

Their storyboard showed a hang glider brightly painted like a large butterfly. This butterfly was shown flying by two girls roller-skating in front of a bank with the French name on the side and cars out front with French license plates. In another scene it showed the glider flying low overtop of motorcycles jumping high off a hill. It also showed the butterfly glider flying low over two girls windsurfing. And finally, landing on a large yellow daisy. They wanted me to pilot the glider for these scenes.

This seemed like quite a bold stunt to perform, but after hearing the payment offered, I accepted the job. So, when the film crew arrived with the butterfly gliders, the all-black outfit with a black motorcycle helmet with black visor, and the director, I was ready for filming.

However, that was a first of many challenges. The director, who was a Frenchman of course, had a very heavy French accent which was a bit challenging to understand. He also had to put a handheld buzzer up to his throat to speak, the result of throat cancer. As you can imagine, it was even more difficult to understand him.

I got David Darling to tow me up with his truck on main street in Kahului. Keep in mind this had to be done safely between cars and power lines. I was in the butterfly glider and flew low over the girls roller-skating by the bank.

The next scene was planned for me to fly over motorcycles as they jumped in the air. The problem was that the director set it up on the down slope of the Haleakala crater. So, after flying low over the jumping motorcycles, I had to land in no wind on the down slope. It was not an easy thing to do, but I somehow managed to pull it off without crashing. By this time, I'm thinking that *THIS DIRECTOR IS GOING TO KILL ME!*

He had no idea what a hang glider was capable of doing and doing it without killing the stunt pilot! And, of course, communicating with him was nearly impossible.

Next came the scene where I needed to fly over the girls' wind surfing. The director set this up on Little Makena Beach. He had hired a local power boat to tow me up off the beach so I could do a low pass over the two girls windsurfing and land back on the beach. It was to be a static line tow which meant the line did not pay out and would tow me a couple hundred feet high, just high enough for me to release from tow, fly low over the girls and land on the beach. When I heard the boat running it sounded like it had a modified cam, and the driver could hardly keep it running.

Bill Moyes had taught me how to do this in Perth, but this time I would be towing from my harness instead of the A Frame. We called it Skyting and it made for much better glider handling. So, with my black outfit and black helmet on (so I looked like the bug part of the butterfly), I hooked into the glider, kicked the sand to signal the boat driver to "hit it". Well, the boat roared, jerked me off the beach just beyond the waves and the engine stalled. I slowly floated down toward the water as the boat driver tried to get the motor to run! Just before hitting the water, I released from the tow line, gasped for a lung full of air, and sank about 15 feet to the sea bottom! Thankfully, I knew not to lock my carabiner to the hang straps, so I quickly unhooked from the hang strap and made a dive for the surface. Unfortunately, the carabiner hooked onto one of the flying wires of the glider and was holding me down.

About this time, two divers with tanks (that were on the boat) grabbed my arms and tried to pull me to the surface. I fought loose, unhooked the carabiner from the flying wire and surfaced just as my lungs felt like they would explode! I was wearing a knee hangar harness so my legs were free to swim, and I swam fast as I could to the beach. I ran up to the director, threw him down on the sand and sat in the middle of him screaming, "You're going to kill me!" I jumped up and walked off the set.

I immediately called Gerard Tevano in France, a pilot I had become friends with at flying comps. Gerard manufactured hang gliders called La Mouette and Cosmos trikes. I asked him to come save me as I felt this crazy French director was going to kill me and I couldn't understand much of what he said. Gerard agreed, after I offered him a sizable reward and a round trip ticket to Hawaii.

Well as luck would have it, that very evening Hurricane Iwa made landfall on the Hawaiian Islands. It was a Category 1 with winds of 80 to 90 miles per hour and wind gusts over 100. It was November 1982. Iwa which means "frigate bird" in Hawaiian was one of the most significant hurricanes of the 20th century to impact the Hawaiian Islands. It caused extensive devastation and disrupted power on the islands of Niihau, Kauai, and Oahu. The damage was more than $300 million which would be $800 million in today's dollars.

Although Maui experienced its adverse impact as well. The entire film crew and I were staying in a pole hotel right on the beach front. Which means the hotel was built up high on like telephone poles. At the height of the storm, my hotel room was rocking and swaying so much I felt like it may go down. Feeling unsafe, I went out to my rental Volkswagen and tied a rope to it and attached it to a nearby palm tree. I rode out the storm safely in the VW, but it was quite a crazy night for sure!

The hotel weathered the storm and once things settled down a couple days later, we were back to filming the commercial. Instead of towing the glider up by boat, we moved down the beach where there was a high enough sand dune next to the water to launch the glider and fly by the girls windsurfing.

The next scene was landing on a giant yellow daisy. It had a yellow round center with green leaves made with welding rods covered with green material. Oh, how perfect -- unyielding welding rods to impale an unsuspecting pilot!

The worst thing about it was that the director placed it right off the end of the road with a 90 degree turn going up to the Haleakala Crater. Just past the daisy was a huge hole caused by a volcano vent tube which had the top broken open. So, if you overshot, you were in the hole of the vent tube. By this time, Gerard had arrived, but I was first to fly. As I made my approach to the daisy with plenty of speed along the paved road, I flared a bit too soon and came down hard on the road just in front of the daisy. I had both hands on the down tubes. When the A frame of the glider smacked the hard pavement it sent a shock to both shoulders. Ouch! Gerard was next, he came in and made a perfect flare landing center of the daisy!

Thank you, Gerard, if you are reading this, you definitely saved me from that crazy director! The director promised to send me a copy of the finished commercial, which I never received. Gee, could it have something to do with me throwing him down on the beach that day? But thankfully, I got paid very well.

Flying Mount Rigi, Switzerland (above).
Unloading gliders from the camper (below).

Chapter 13
More Flying in Europe and Off to Ireland

I returned to Tegelberg for another flight. I decided to mount my 35 mm camera with wide angle lens to the wing of the Firebird so I could get photos of flying around the Neuschwanstein Castle.

I camped at the bottom near the lift to get an early ride up in time to set up the glider and mount the camera and release system before the thermals started popping. It was a beautiful day with a high cloud base. On that day, none of the pilots were able to soar above launch. They were able to scratch around below launch, but they simply could not find enough lift to rise above launch.

After watching for a while, I decided to fly before the wind direction changed because I wanted to get pictures of flying around the castle. After a clean launch I headed straight toward the castle so I would be high enough to make a couple circles and get some good shots. I remember a group of people out in the courtyard yelling and waving at me. I waved back and headed out to the landing area near the bottom of the tram.

When I was about 500 feet above the landing, I flew into a huge thermal. My variometer (an instrument used by hang glider pilots to measure the lift in feet per minute with a visual graph and an audio beeping tone) started singing. The nose of the glider popped up and I put it in a sharp turn to stay in the lift. I was able to circle round and round just like the hawks and eagles I had watched in Montana. The vario was pegged, (meaning it was measuring maximum lift) and singing loudly. I remember seeing bits of hay and bugs rising in the thermal with me. I was way out front of the launch and climbed right up to cloud base which was about 2000 feet above the launch. I could see a couple gliders below the launch, and they were just scratching around on the rock face. Next to the launch, I could see the awe inspiring majestic peaks of the Alps. They seemed to go on and on for as far as you could see. The alpine lakes nestled in between the mountains glistened in the sun. It was breathtaking!

I decided to travel to Ireland after that. I journeyed across the sea with my camper on a huge hovercraft ferry that had four engines (one on each corner). It was an amazing craft. When I got to Ireland the sun was shining and it was beautifully green. The people kept saying "particularly nice day." I thought it was a local greeting at first, but then realized it really was indeed "unusually nice weather" because they said it rains a lot in Ireland. While there, I noticed they were cutting sod from the ground that they used for fuel in their stoves. I had seen this practice in movies before, but it was great to witness locals firsthand as they cut their sod.

I fondly remember the great pubs with plenty of Guinness beer. At the entrance to some of the pubs, there were two doors. If you were dressed decently and with a lady, you went through the door to the right. If you were just off from work, or there to have some pints and songs with your lads, you went through the door on the left. I don't know why, but I just marveled at that concept.

I traveled along the East coastline where I found a nice campground along the sea cliffs. It was just spectacular! The next day, I watched seabirds soaring above the cliffs and sea and realized it was totally soarable with a steady 10 to 15 mph wind blowing straight into the cliffs.

"Is it flyable I asked myself?" I estimated the cliffs to be around 200 to 300 feet high. It seemed just like the conditions in Hawaii, so I unloaded the Firebird and set it up. I could hear murmurs of chatter from the campers, and I know they were thinking I was crazy. I talked one of them into wiring me off, which means they hold the glider nose wires steady into the wind on the cliff's edge. I told him to listen for my command to let go and then he was to dive to the ground as I pushed off and climbed up and away. And there I was, soaring above their heads with the seabirds on the cliffs of Ireland.

I flew back and forth along the cliff for about an hour. When ready to land I flew away from the cliffs' edge, back behind the rotor, and did a smooth landing. Based on their faces, the easy landing without some sort of crash was much to everyone's surprise. There were quite a few people touring on bicycles in the camp and we all had a fun time around the campfire that night enjoying some more Guinness.

I stayed in Ireland about a month and enjoyed the variety of campgrounds. I had a bit of a scary experience while driving through Dublin, though. There was fighting going on in the streets with gangs of people. At one point a bunch of them started pushing on the side of the camper. It felt as though they were going to tip it over, so I just down shifted and gunned straight ahead knocking several of them out of the way. I didn't stop until I was out of the city. I felt immensely lucky not to have had a worse outcome.

I then traveled by ferry back to mainland Europe and on to Paris, France. The streets of Paris are lined out like a giant wagon wheel with the streets leading to the city center like spokes. I drove the camper into an underground parking garage at a nice hotel and checked in. I was ready for a camping break and excited to check out the famous French cuisine.

I stayed for two weeks because I really wanted to see ALL of Paris. Of course, one of the first stops was The Eiffel Tower. I bought a loaf of French bread and a nice bottle of French wine and headed out on a city adventure. There was a nice park nearby with other people who had the same idea. The restaurant at the top of the Tower was being remodeled, so I had dinner at the restaurant about midway up. The food was delicious!

Of course, being in Paris, I also went to see the Louvre. While standing in line, I saw none other than Wolfman Jack (a very popular radio personality from the '70s) wearing a large black western hat full of stick pins. Of course, that voice was unmistakable, and he was being quite boisterous. We talked and he invited me to the Moulin Rouge that night and even gave me an admission ticket. The Louvre was amazing, and I spent the whole day there and still didn't see it all. I could have easily spent another day or two there to truly appreciate the art and exhibits.

At the Moulin Rouge that night, Wolfman had been drinking and was quite loud, so I distanced myself from him and his group right away. The show was great with many beautiful topless dancers.

The French like to do their main dining in the early afternoon so I bought a tailored suit so I could go to the nicer restaurants. I marveled at how they lined tables up against the walls and then pulled them out so you could slide in. They then were able to efficiently serve you from the front.

Many times, you ended up setting next to a complete stranger which just added to the experience. One day I was sitting next to a distinguished looking French gentleman. I decided to point to the menu as I didn't speak French. Once the meal was delivered, I tried to match the way he handled his silverware. Shortly thereafter, he turned toward me and said in broken English, "and so where in America are you from". Obviously, I was pretty darn easy to spot!

A great surprise happened when I went to the movie theater with friends and saw the Wrigley's commercial of me flying from Mt. Cook on the big screen. I don't think they showed it at theaters in the U.S. Of course, the gum wrapper was different as it was one of the international commercials. That was the first and only time I saw the commercial while in Europe.

I then traveled to the Interlaken area of Switzerland to fly the popular hang gliding site on Mt. Rigi. The pilots transport their gliders to the mountain top on the clacker train. It was a charming train that also carried goods to people in the small villages on the mountain. It is a spectacular place to fly with beautiful green fields to land in at the base near a quaint little village on a beautiful lake.

Much to my surprise, I was fortunate to find a very nice and clean campground. I was able to leave my tent that attached to the camper by simply zipping it closed. I stayed at that site for nearly two weeks as the flying was so good.

The rest of the summer was dedicated to flying sites all around Europe. One that I particularly enjoyed was at Lake Como in Italy. It was nice because launch was on a grassy knoll at the end of the lake. When the wind blew straight up the face, you could land on top like flyers could do on Bald Hill in Australia. I ended up selling the two Firebird Gliders there as the summer was coming to an end.

The next stop was back to Innsbrook where I left the camper with my friend Martha Zec. I then flew back to Hawaii for the winter season.

I went back to Europe the next year for another summer of hang gliding in the Alps. At the end of that summer, I shipped the camper to the U.S. You could easily do this, because the shipping cost was covered by VW Hawaii as part of the overseas delivery purchase plan. I spent a total of 17 months traveling the world and flying the highest hang gliding mountain sites.

Chapter 14
Back to the U.S.A.

Once back in Hawaii, I heard about a new glider design by Roy Haggard of Ultralight Products known as UP. Pete Brock, famous for his work in auto design including the Corvette Stingray, owned the company. The glider was called the Comet. It was outperforming all other gliders on the market at that time, so I bought one. It had a floating crossbar which really helped in handling and made climbing in the lift of a thermal much easier. It also had a great glide. I loved that new glider. It was especially nice when the conditions were good for going down range along the "green wall" on Oahu. Its performance worked well for hours of floating along in the ridge lift of the trade winds along the coast.

In the summer of 1986, while flying in the CanAm Challenge off Mt. Swansea in Invermere B.C., I met Shirley Jones up on launch. After getting to know each other over the two weeks of competition and partying in the evenings (the Canadians sure know how to do that), Shirley joined me on an adventure trip to camp throughout the Baja Peninsula of Mexico for the winter.

I had just purchased a new Toyota pickup and topper with camping gear, two hang gliders, an inflatable raft and motor, a wind surfing board and sail, and a surfboard. Of course, all the toys were strapped to the rack on top. It turned into five months of camping on different beaches, and we ended up in Cabo San Lucas.

One great memory was of a bar at the Finisterre Resort called Whale Watchers. It was right above the cliffs near Land's End and the prevailing Pacific Ocean wind blew right up the face. It was a perfect place to launch a hang glider. However, there was no place to land below the bar. It was a sheer cliff reaching down to the crashing waves of the Pacific Ocean. You simply had to get enough lift to take you to a beach about two miles away.

Well, I had to try it. Shirley and I carried the glider on our shoulders right through the bar dodging people enjoying drinks and watching whales. There was just enough room to set up at the edge of the bar and fly the glider off the cliff. The bar patrons thought they were going to witness a crazy man commit suicide and it drew quite a crowd ready to drink and watch the spectacle. Thankfully, the wind was consistent and strong enough to carry me up and out over the rock cliffs. I was able to soar back and forth in front of the bar and made it back to the beach for a safe landing. Whew, that one had my heart thumping quite a bit.

While soaring above the prestigious cliff houses on the Pedregal, I flew by a couple setting out on their veranda. We shouted out hello's as they stood there in amazement. The man came down to the beach once I landed to ask about hang gliding. He invited Shirley and me up to his beautiful home for lunch. We had a nice time and thought that would be it. However, we ended up meeting them on a flight to mainland Mexico a month later. They said they had been trying to locate us as they wanted to know if Shirley and I could house sit for them. Well, that was an easy YES! We were fortunate enough to house sit there for two years.

Shirley and I got married the following summer, followed by the birth of our son, Christopher. At that point we were in Calgary where the 1988 Winter Olympics were being held. Since Christopher was born there during that time, I always called him my Olympic Kid.

Shortly thereafter, we moved to Grants Pass, Oregon, where my brother, Gary, and his family lived. He said it was a good place to raise a family, so I bought land and had a house built. Our second son, Timothy, was born a year and a half later. Both boys eventually enjoyed flying on many tandem flights with me.

Of course, there was a flying site nearby called Bald Hill and we could see it out of our front window. There also was another flying site nearby called Woodrat Mountain. I met many hang gliding pilots there, including Russ Camp. Russ asked me to take his mother on a tandem flight from Bald Hill for her birthday and he joined us in air in his glider. We had a great flight together. Russ told me recently that his mom always talked about how much she enjoyed the experience. I have always loved introducing people to the joys of flying tandem in a hang glider.

Around this time, I met Dan Buchanan who was a paraplegic and wanted to experience flight in a hang glider. My neighbor, Bill Woods, was an accomplished hot air balloon pilot, so I asked him if he would take Dan and me on a tandem flight strapped under his balloon. He said sure and we set it all up.

On that day, there was a film crew from the local Medford TV news that covered the flight. There was one cameraman in the balloon basket and another filming from the ground. We used an automobile tow strap to attach the glider at its CG point to the basket We also had a line with a three-ring-circus release attached to my down tube. We then tied the balloon basket to my truck bumper. Once the balloon rose above the glider and the straps were tight, the balloon pilot released the line to the truck.

Dan and I could hear the blast of the propane fire as the balloon lifted us off the ground. The scariest part of the whole experience was in the first part of the lift off, when I knew we didn't have enough altitude to release and make a safe landing. But all went well.

Grants Pass is at 540 feet above sea level. The balloon slowly climbed to around 12,500 feet (or a mile high) in no wind. I had radio contact with the balloon pilot and when I said we were ready to fly, he put the balloon in a 900 foot per minute descent. I pulled the nose of the glider down in a steep dive, released and we flew smoothly away from the balloon.

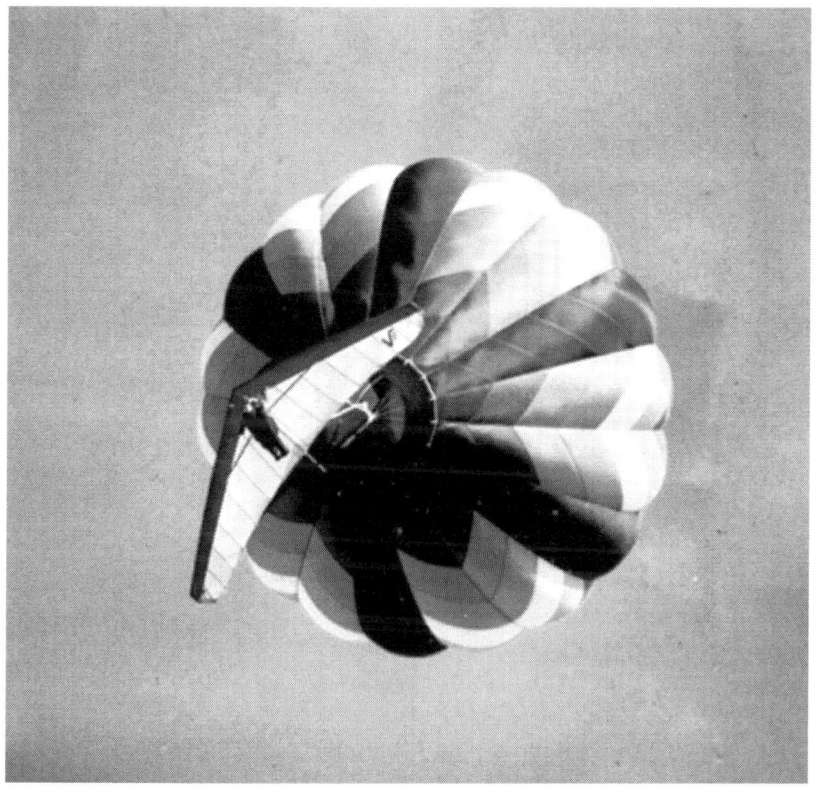

Tandem balloon drop in Oregon.

I had attached smoke bombs to each corner of the glider A frame that I set off just before releasing from the balloon to signal the cameraman on the ground that we were ready to fly. He got great footage. However, the cameraman in the basket got spooked when Bill put the balloon in the descent for the release. He sat down in the basket and totally missed the release sequence. After releasing, I was able to circle around the balloon with smoke pouring off the glider. The cameraman in the basket was then able to

91

get footage of us circling the balloon. The ground cameraman got Dan and I coming in for a perfect landing on the wheels that I had attached to the glider base tube. The smoke still coming off the glider made for a great showing on the local news that evening.

I will never forget Dan's yahoo's and the look of joy on his face during the flight. Dan decided he wanted to learn to fly hang gliders, so I sold him his first hang glider that had red lightning bolts sewn onto each wing of the sail. It also had landing wheels attached for him to land on.

We would toss Dan into the air at our Woodrat flying site while he laid prone in his harness. He, then, was like any other pilot soaring in the air. Dan moved to San Francisco and did a lot of flying from an ocean cliff soaring site called Fort Funston. At that location, you could land on top close to the launch and parking lot which worked very well for Dan. I traveled to Fort Funston several times to fly with Dan and the other pilots who frequented the site.

Several years later, Dan got a great gig of opening air shows with a routine where he towed up with a winch and line attached to a small pickup. He had designed a Class B fireworks system that was attached to his glider. He also had an American Flag attached to his king post to add to the opening show drama. He would start the air shows with the National Anthem playing to the crowd. Dan became well-known at air shows all over the world. Unfortunately, in June of 2018, Dan encountered a strong wind gust on landing that flipped his glider upside down and he was killed in the accident. Dan had been flying air shows for decades at that point. RIP my hang gliding friend Dan Buchanan.

One of the most beautiful places I flew at that time was Yosemite National Park in Northeastern California. We flew from Glacier Point off the steep rockface with Half Dome in the background. My guide and fellow hang glider pilot was Eves Tall Chief. Eves had flown more than 300 flights from Glacier Point. We were required to launch our gliders before 9 a.m. to avoid collisions with tourists in the meadow where we landed. It was a spectacular flight that took us in the water spray of Yosemite Falls which was such an incredible rush. Hang glider pilots from all around the world came to experience this awe-inspiring natural wonder.

Chapter 15
Designing a Water Gliding Boat Tow Operation

In 1994, I attended the World Hang Gliding Competition in the Owens Valley, CA. It was an exciting experience because it was the first World Hang Gliding Competition to be held in the United States. I think there were 36 countries competing for the championships. It was there that I met Jim Zeiset, the U.S. Hang Gliding Association president. He was also the "Meet Head" (which meant he oversaw the competition).

The Owens Valley is known as the "big air" flying site in the U.S. because of the strong thermals that can take you to cloud base at 1000-feet-per minute. It is a special place to me because I made a personal all-time altitude gain flying off Gunter's 12,000 foot launch.

I was flying with Jim and his Green Team one practice day when I was able to reach 20,200 feet above sea level while flying with oxygen. At that altitude, I went for a long glide above the Inyo Mountains. I announced to Jim and the team "it's so beautiful! I can see sparkles on the ice crystals in the air." Jim came back on the radio and said, "Combs check your oxygen!" I looked down at the oxygen toggle switch mounted just above the emergency parachute on my harness chest -- and it was in the OFF position. You can't smell the oxygen and when I bent over waiting to launch, the switch must have inadvertently been switched off. After landing, I noticed my fingernails had taken on a slight blue color. A couple other pilots also said my lips were blue. I had a splitting headache the rest of the day. But I was stoked!

I had been dreaming of making a hang gliding boat towing system and had made several computer drawings for such a system. I showed them to Jim, and he said, "let's build it!" He was an aeronautical engineer and had a nice shop at his ranch in Salida, Colorado. After the meet, we headed to Jim's ranch and then flew in his 320 Cessna to Lake Havasu City, AZ., to buy a Magic Catamaran hull boat.

When the Magic was built, we took it back to his shop in Colorado. Jim was a very good welder and we started making the hang gliding tow boat of my dreams. It was quite a performance boat with a big block 503 MerCruiser engine that put out 415 prop shaft horsepower, and a Bravo Three Counter rotating twin prop outdrive. The cat hull could do 50 MPH on the water. We needed that kind of speed because sometimes, when under tow, the glider can get into sinking air, and it is imperative to maintain the climb by powering through this air.

The boat had a hinged six-foot-long "flight deck" on the back that was controlled up and down by Hydraulic rams from MerCruiser. It had a hydraulic winch system that Jim designed with a narrow spool that carried around 3500 feet of tow line. For line retrieval, after the glider was released, we used a fighter jet emergency pilot ejection parachute attached at the end of the line at the glider. I found it in an Army/Navy store. I shortened the bridal lines a bit and it would fly steady on rewind after releasing from the glider somewhere around half-a-mile high or 2500 feet. The winch was smooth under tow, not jerky like autobrake controlled winches that were being used on land towing systems at that time.

We originally used pontoons from a river raft for glider floats. I later designed floats that, when aired up, were flat on the bottom and top. I got the idea from the flat bottoms used on self-bailing river rafts. They skimmed to a stop when landing on the water, rather than digging in like the round ones.

I also designed a stackable tandem harness system that worked much better than side-by-side systems that were commonly used at the time. The stackable system gave the pilot much more room in the control A frame. In fact, you wouldn't even know there was another person in the glider with you if you didn't turn around and look above you. There were handles sewn into the side of the pilot's harness for the tandem passenger to hold onto. Betty Rothman of High Energy Sports in L.A. made them up for me. The stackable tandem harness system became popular for aerotowing operations and at least one boat towing operation and they are still used today.

I decided to name our boat tow system "WaterGlide". Jim and I introduced the "WaterGlide" Boat Towing System at the Women's World Hang Gliding Championships in Lake Chelan, Washington. I remember doing a tandem tow up near the launch site. After releasing from tow, I hooked a thermal that carried us up and above the launch. Later, the launch director accused me of showing the American woman's team where the thermals were. So, we didn't do that again.

We took the WaterGlide boat back to Lake Havasu and I was able to secure a commercial operation doing tandem tows out of the Nautical Inn Resort on the island. While there, we were contacted by the National Geographic Society to do a segment on their popular "Next Step" TV show. I got to take Dara Torres, the Olympic Swimmer and 12-time Olympic medalist, for a flight on the Water Glider. She was a kick. While filming the launch off the back of the boat she said, "Oh, I think Robert will know I'm back here alright with these sharp fingernails."

After a year of operating the Magic Catamaran "WaterGlide" boat and understanding some improvements that could be made to the system, I wanted to build another upgraded model of boat. Jim was getting very busy with his plant band business in Colorado, and he wanted to concentrate on that business, so we dissolved our partnership.

I went to Commercial Water Sports in Lake Havasu, the largest manufacturer of platform-launched parasail boats. They were building a ridged inflatable with a 31-foot monohull design that had large inflatable tubes on the sides. I believed this design would be much more stable on the water for the "WaterGlide" operation, so I had them custom build one for me. I used the same power system as the Magic because that engine and outdrive was working well, but I upgraded the hydraulic winch system.

About that time, I discovered Spectra fabric tow line. It used an 1/8-inch Spectra line with a 7,000-pound test. The Spectra featured hollow braid line that did not stretch, would float and was impervious to oil. It was perfect for tow line.

I took a large ocean fishing reel and 2 feet of 1/8-inch Spectra line to the machine shop that built winches for Commercial Water Sports Parasail boats. I asked the owner if he could build a level-winder reel that could carry 6,000 feet of Spectra line. The owner was familiar with the 'WaterGlide" operation and had an interest in my project, so he took on the challenge. He even let me come to his shop in the evenings and allowed me to help with menial jobs while he made up the custom reel. He had a C&C machine that would make the different aluminum parts and then had them triple anodized. It was great fun as I kind of had a mechanical mind anyway and loved learning how to make the different parts. The new hydraulic winch system worked fantastic in the new boat design.

It took three people to operate the "WaterGlide" system. We had the pilot, a licensed captain, and a winch operator, who was always a pretty girl in a bikini called the "winch wench" for fun. The parasail operation at the Nautical Inn used off duty firemen who had their boat captain's licenses. We also hired them for the WaterGlide operation.

Jim Hoover, owner of the water sports concession, became my partner. Wendell Smith (a fireman) and Jim Hoover were also partners in the operation.

My two young sons, Christopher and Timothy, helped make it a family business by selling bottles of cold water to passengers for a dollar a bottle while on the boat. The air temps could reach 110-plus degrees in Havasu, so the cool water was always a great refresher. The boys had a good time watching all the wild girls on the party boats. I told them not to tell their mom everything they saw!

About the same time, Dan Johnson of Hang Gliding Magazine did an article on the WaterGlide operation. It was a nice surprise to open the magazine and see the story along with a photo of my young son, Tim, and me in the stackable harness preparing for a flight.

One of the special aspects of the operation was that with 6,000-feet of Spectra tow line, we were able to do a mile-high tow to 5,200 feet. We rarely towed this high as a typical tow was to 2,500 feet. But, one year, we did this with a local radio announcer doing a live broadcast from the glider during the Fourth of July celebration. When I released the glider from the tow, I had two smoke bombs pouring smoke from the glider making it an exciting and memorable sight. Then, on landing approach, I flew under the center arch of the London bridge. I had acquired permission from the Havasu police department to block off traffic on the bridge -- just allowing foot traffic and the bridge was packed. I had to go through the center arch with a lot of air speed so I could pull up on the other side of the bridge and then turn around in the harness and wave to the crowd. After that, I floated down to a soft landing on the water canal. It was a hit, and we were slammed with people who wanted to fly in the Water Glider.

The operation was such a success that I took it to the Miami Boat Show in Florida. Much to my surprise, I got three orders for the boats and systems. One went to Cabo San Lucas, so I got to go there to train the required Mexican pilot, Ernesto Mogana, on the system. It was a beautiful place to fly in the Cabo Bay at Land's End. Ernesto now operates a successful trike tour business in Cabo San Lucas.

The WaterGlide boat was also a hit in Cabo. The owners had a silent Mexican partner which allowed them to operate in Mexico. The company also had a parasail boat operation with a sales booth right on the beach where people could buy flights. We also sold flights on the Water Glider from the booth.

Over time, the Water Glider became so popular that three other Mexican parasail operations complained to the Harbor Master about the American-run WaterGlide boat getting an unfair amount of business. We all had to pay the Harbor Master what is called "Mordida" just to operate. The "Mordida" fee kept going up for our Water Glide operation and we even received life threats from the other operators. Obviously, we took the threats seriously. Eventually, they decided to convert the WaterGlide boat to a parasail boat to preserve the peace ... and life!

The second boat went to Marco Island, Florida, and the third went to Hilton Head, South Carolina.

I also showed at the Sun & Fun Air Show in Lakeland, Florida. As part of the purchase price, I included training. Wills Wing Hang Gliders in Los Angeles custom built the 220 Falcon with stronger leading edges. The addition of floats and mounting hardware added a bit more weight and stress on the air frame than the glider was originally made for, so they upgraded it.

Later, I was able to get a water sports concession on Captiva Island, Florida, at the South Seas Plantation Resort. It is a stunning location in the Gulf of Mexico. It became extremely popular as guests just walked up to the activity booth where they could book all water sports, including parasailing, windsurfing, jet skis, etc. They showed their resort card and lined up on the dock for a flight.

We would take three people on the boat at a time because we could do three flights to 2,500 feet in an hour. It took about five minutes to tow the glider to altitude and a 10 minute glide down to the water. We then simply lowered the flight deck to the water, winched the glider with pilot and passenger up on the flight deck, raised the flight deck, hooked the nose of the glider to the mast, lowered the flight deck to level, changed out passengers, and it was "go to cruise" with the next one.

The boat captain would point the boat into the wind and go to full throttle. When the wind meter showed 35 mph, I would release the glider and it would lift off the flight deck in a rush (most of the girls would let out a cry of excitement) to 30 or 40 feet. It would then climb in smooth line payout to around 2,500 feet or half a mile high.

When the winch operator saw a red mark on the line appear she would notify the boat captain who would then cut the power and turn the boat 180 degrees back toward me reducing the tow line tension. Then I was able to do a smooth release from tow. The parachute at the end of the tow line which was kept closed by the line tension would snap open and the "wench winch" would start the rewind. The winch with the level winder would rewind the line at an amazing 80 to 90 mph back onto the reel.

When all line was rewound back on the reel, the winch rewind would stop, and the parachute would land on the flight deck. I was able to make this happen by placing a steel needle bearing inside the hollow braid spectra line in just the right spot (with plenty of trial and error). When the bearing in the line passed through an electric feeler switch it would shut the rewind down and the parachute would land on the flight deck every time.

It really worked well and kept the parachute from accidentally being sucked down the mast and roller bearings. In this way we were always ready to go for the next flight without delay.

Everyone loved the experience. It was so popular there that the concession owner, who had two new parasail boats, gave us the boot after our season contract. I offered him the opportunity to become partners in the "WaterGlide" boat operation, but he said, "It's too popular and you're getting too many of my parasail customers." He recommended I come back and see him after he paid off his new parasail boats.

I decided to take my boat to North Carolina and started flying for John Harris of Kitty Hawk Kites. I flew out of Hatteras in the Outer Banks. John owns one of the longest running hang gliding schools, if not the longest, in the United States. Kitty Hawk, of course, is where the Wright Brothers made powered flight fame.

The other boat, that was operating in Florida, also came up to the Outer Banks and worked out of Duck Island on the northern end of the Outer Banks where John also had an outdoor kite store. John was a great guy to work with and we had a lot of fun flying there. I often flew to the southern end of the Banks to Ocracoke Island and would land in the small bay. It was beautiful!

After returning to Lake Havasu and flying out of the Nautical Inn, we started towing the glider up through the Topock Canyon Gorge on the Colorado River. We took six passengers and lunch for everyone. We also picked up people from the Sand Bar that was the hot spot for boat parties. It was a spectacular flight through the canyon. I had to be careful not to catch the tow line on the canyon walls while navigating some of the sharper turns on the river.

One memorable moment was a flight with a quite inebriated young girl. While getting close to release altitude, the glider suddenly pitched up in a strong thermal. Almost immediately, the tow line tightened straight down to the boat, and the weak link that I kept in the end of the tow line behind the drogue chute snapped. There was so much pressure on the line that when the weak link snapped, the glider shot straight up into a stall, then pitched over and almost straight down. The girl who had been screeching with joy (remember she was a bit inebriated), let out a blood curdling scream! I knew it was all fine as the glider flew out of the stall, but I got so tickled at the sound of her scream that I couldn't quit laughing. I know that wasn't very nice of me, but I just couldn't help it! Normally we refrained from taking passengers that had too much to drink.

Another time, a guy asked me to show him how I could circle up in a thermal. There was always plenty of thermal updrafts along the desert shores of Lake Havasu, so I did it and he got very quiet ... and then vomited all over me as, of course, I was right below him.

I had been working on the WaterGlide project for almost five years at that point. It was a labor intensive job because, in addition to flying five to six hours and dealing with customers, I had to clean, fuel and service the boat at the end of every day. And then there was folding up the glider and putting it away. Our only days off were poor weather days which there weren't many. I also handled an occasional all-night job of changing out a broken outdrive or other engine problem. We ran the engine pretty hard all day. And just the maintenance of the Big Block MerCruiser engine was a job. I started thinking about my next great flying adventure.

Tandem launch off the WaterGlide boat.

Chapter 16
A Great Story in Hang Gliding Magazine

My friend Dan Johnson wrote an article in Hang Gliding Magazine about my Water Gliding Operation in the December 1998 issue. Dan has been writing hang gliding, Light Sport Trike and Light Sport Aircraft reviews for many years and is well respected for his work by the flying community. Dan has given me permission to reprint his article here. I am grateful as I could not have said it better! Many thanks to you Dan.

GET IN,

GET UP

(AND HOPEFULLY)

GET THE

BUG!

Robert Combs' Water Gliding Operation Could Bring
Hang Gliding to Tourist Resorts Worldwide

You may have seen it before, back when USHGA Director Jim Zeiset was associated with an early development for an intriguing new flight training system. Now some years later, the project has reached a much higher state of the art and is ready for sales and operation.

WATER GLIDERS, PART II

The subject is Water Gliders, the brainchild of entrepreneur Robert Combs. He has created, built and refined a purpose-built and self-contained watercraft that can tow a hang glider up with two aboard. Intended for training flights at tourist destinations, the Water Gliders system is a sophisticated conglomeration of commercial equipment that is the best I have seen 25 years of observing such developments.

It works like this: Take a specially configured boat, add a modern hang glider with a qualified instructor, plus trained boat operator, and you have a package that may compete nicely against those ubiquitous parasailing operations one can see virtually at any beachside tourist destination in the world. Three Water Gliders boats are currently in operation (one in Cabo San Lucas, Mexico; one at Outer Banks, North Carolina going to Key West for winter 98; one going to the South Seas Plantation at Captiva Island, Florida) and reviews after a year's activity are very positive.

DEDICATED DEVELOPER

Combs has dedicated himself to this project with a zeal and enthusiasm that is positively infectious. Within minutes of conversation with him, would-be pilots are ready to strap themselves to the glider.

Even more amazing is how quickly he can convert hotel operators who ask to see nitty-gritty details of the potential for revenue generation.

In both cases, substantial resistance must be overcome, and with no surprise. Tourists—or occurrent pilots—are typically at first reluctant to go aloft in an aircraft that seems foreign to their prior experience. Many initially think they must go solo. Combs is quick to reassure them that they'll go dual. Further, with his comforting professional demeanor, Combs explains that he will be their instructor. This, in addition to the impressive construction of the boat and tow mechanisms, sways many tourists into going aloft.

Hotel operators are another breed. While a surprising number of them have been convinced to take a flight as part of their evaluation, they are usually hardheaded businessmen looking to make a profit while limiting their liability.

Liability in most forms of aviation is presumed, yet Combs has found ways to address this concern. He has secured insurance which is not always available to aviation enterprises. He has the credentials to do what he does. But it is just as often the competent execution of the boat rig itself that closes the deal.

You probably know Robert Combs, although you may not recognize his name. Nearly 20 years ago the Wrigley's chewing gum Company selected Rob from a large group of candidates to star in a series of commercials (one national and two international). In each clip he flies his hang glider from scenic precipices after first enjoying a stick of gum. The commercials aired for three years in the single longest running promotion ever for the company.

IMPRESSIVE POTENTIAL

Just as Disney spend millions on new rides or attractions each year, resort operators also seek new ways to entertain their guests. They've added water slides, golf courses and in-pool bars to provide a new spark for their businesses. Along comes Combs with his Water Gliders operation and you can almost see the wheels turning in their brains.

He successfully penetrated the very upscale resort of South Seas Plantation on Florida's Captiva Island (near Sanibel and Ft. Meyers). Here

102

guests could sign up via the activity's booth, pay by charging to their rooms, and go for a thrill of a lifetime over the calm, clear, blue water surrounding the island. Business was brisk until the huge resort was sold to a new owner who wanted to evaluate all the concessions including the Water Gliders operation. While this transition went on Combs and his rig traveled north to the Outer. Banks of North Carolina.

This popular East Coast tourist destination has hosted two Water Gliders boats all summer, and Combs reports very satisfying business during the summer of 1998. One boat was operated by Combs; the other is owned and operated by Doug Wanda of Adrenaline Water Gliding. The two rigs picked this particular destination thanks to an arrangement with Kitty Hawk Kites.

As all Hang Gliding readers know, Kitty Hawk Kites is one of the largest hang gliding schools in the world, and the company operates eight retail stores around the Nags Head area where the Wright Brothers first flew. After 25 years in the business, owner John Harris knows what works to satisfy tourists, and he quickly jumped on the Water Gliders Band Wagon.

THE WATER GLIDERS BOAT

A large V-hulled craft with a flat floor like a deck boat is the heart of the Water Gliders rig. It is ringed with a large and extremely durable inflatable collar that assures a very stable environment even at launch speeds of 30+ mph and in waters that aren't particularly smooth. The large boat (see specifications) has a 502 cubic inch, multiport, fuel-injected V8 marine engine that pushes the beast through the water with great enthusiasm, partly thanks to dual counter-rotating props. Her captain is stationed at midships along with a winch operator who doubles as a "mate," as she helps student pilots don their life vests and gets them in their flight harnesses. Impressive as the boat is, the more custom development may be the winch system.

Combs' first boat was more a high-powered houseboat than the capable machine shown in the accompanying photos. And the winch system on that prototype—through very sleekly mounted under the deck below a heavy plexiglass viewport—was no match for the sophisticated final version. Now, an all-hydraulic system smoothly pays out the line at a pre-set tension. This system allows the boat to authoritatively tow aloft the glider and its two occupants with no line jerking or vibration imparted.

Since the instructor and student can easily attain altitudes of 2,000 to 3,000 feet before release to start a gliding free flight, a lengthy towline is suddenly left high in the sky. To prevent the line from merely falling into the water—perhaps atop other watercraft scurrying about underneath—the winch hydraulically tows the line back to the boat at a dizzyingly fast pace. It is held totally out of the water by a parachute strung on the line near the link with the glider. Under tow the parachute is being pulled backwards so it remains collapsed, opening only as the pilot releases the line and the winch operator hauls it back to the boat.

WINGS OVER THE WATER

The hang glider is ordinary enough: the popular Wills Wing Falcon 225. However, it is fitted with a set of inflatable floats based on the same welded-seam construction as the boat collar, all secured by a sturdy dual-strut system. The floats and struts were designed and tested extensively by Combs over the last few years. Despite the large size of the floats, the Falcon can regularly sustain a 10-minute flight before returning to the surface. Though limited duration is what most new flyers prefer, much longer flights are possible in convective lift conditions. Landings are easy and smooth, as though landing on giant airbags.

Another improvement from the earlier craft is the rear "flight deck." Once instructor and pilot have safely landed—commonly to loud expressions of delight from the passenger—they float in the water without disconnecting themselves. The Water Gliders boat quickly approaches the pair and throws a V-bridal to the hang glider. After lining up the boat and glider, the boat captain lowers the rear deck and pulls the glider and its occupants up on board. Powerful hydraulic pistons raise the deck and the student is free to exit his harness.

As the recently-landed student joins the other customers for soft drinks and snacks aboard the comfortable Water Gliders deck, another student is prepared for a flight and process starts all over again. Boat captain, winch operator, and instructor work as a team in delivering safe flying enjoyment that has never failed to excite, says Combs.

Passengers are always students of course. As an approved instructor through USHGA, Combs is very careful to sign up each student as a member. This accomplishes several goals.

SAFE AND PROPER

Through USHGA'S FAA-sanctioned program, Combs can legally deliver flight training as part of an exemption to FAR Part 103 despite the for-profit environment. Though certainly drawing students for the thrill and entertainment value, the Water Gliders program is entirely legal and perfectly legitimate as training. In fact, Combs refers all students to hang gliding schools in their home area so those who desire can continue their instruction, perhaps ending up as solo hang glider pilots.

As with any proper training school, Combs is fastidious about safety. He uses helmets and a ballistic parachute, teaches according to an accredited syllabus, carefully follows well-established safety procedures, uses highly trained assistants, and has the proper USHGA credentials to perform tandem training. His equipment is topnotch, and his attitude is serious, although he never loses sight of the fact that this is about fun. Nonetheless, fun includes no alcohol or drugs aboard his tightly run ship.

Unless adverse forces prevail, Combs' work over the last decade could produce a fleet of Water Gliders, with operations springing up in many popular tourist destinations like the Caribbean or Mexico, plus spots all over the U.S. If so, and if tourists enjoy the thrill of flight, they can check out an operation near a vacation destination. Resort operators are inquiring regularly and it may not be long before you'll see a Water Gliders operation many places you see parasailing.

SPECIFICATIONS

Boat Length ....…...................…...…......36 ft. (overall, with flight deck)
Boat Width ………………………….…....……………13 ft.(see note below)
Boat Capacity ………………………….……………6 persons + crew of three*
Engine …………………………………...........…….415 hp, MerCruiser brand
Winch Line Capacity …………………...…....……6,000 ft. 1/8-inch spectra)
Hang Glider ……………….......………....…..........Wills Wing Falcon
Hang Glider Float Size …........…………....……...…................…… 12 ft. long

Note: The inflatable collar can be deflated for transportation by trailer, making the width 9.5 ft. which is considered road legal.

*Captain, pilot, winch operator or "mate" assist with life vests.

GET IN, GET UP

(AND HOPEFULLY)

GET THE BUG!

by Dan Johnson

Robert Combs' Water Gliding Operation Could Bring Hang Gliding to Tourist Resorts Worldwide

The young boy in the photo is Robert's son Timothy, around 7 years old.

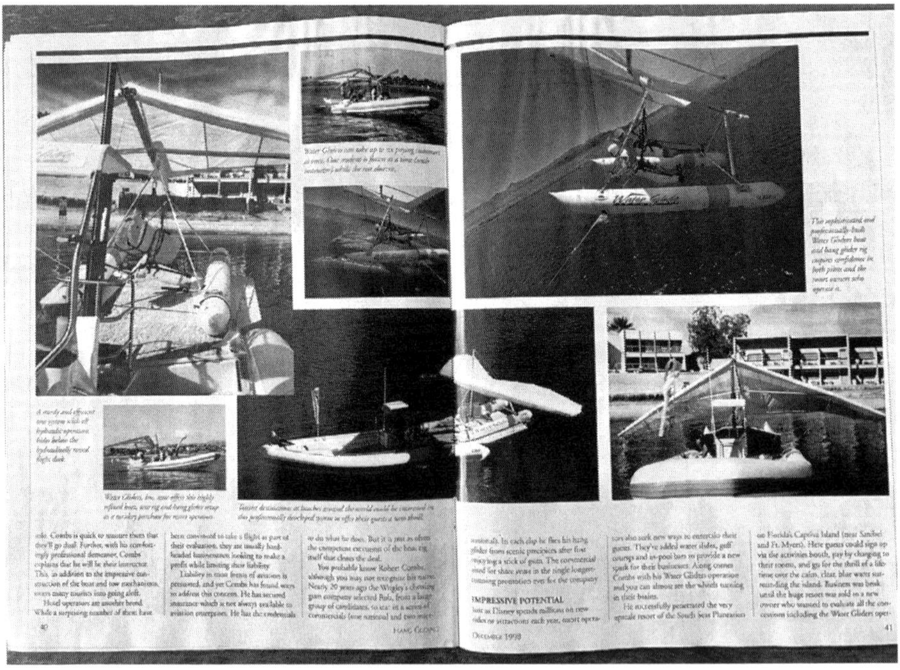

Chapter 17
Starting a Trike Operation

It was about this time in 2003 when Gerry Charlesbois from Kauai, Hawaii, visited us in Lake Havasu. I knew Gerry from flying hang gliders with him on Oahu and had seen him at different hang gliding meets around the U.S. He had a commercial ultralight trike operation on Kauai, and he needed a second licensed instructor pilot so he could take couples and friends on flights with two aircraft. I fit the bill and I really longed to get back to Hawaii.

The great thing about this tandem trike flying option was that it only required one person as instructor-pilot to take up a paying customer. My operation at that time required three people -- the pilot, boat captain, and the required spotter or winch operator. The WaterGlider also required a lot more maintenance work, so I decided to give Kauai a try. My oldest son, Chris, came along as he could help as ground crew.

Gerry said he had a film job in Oahu and needed me to take over the flying while he was away. The plan was for him to be away for about two weeks and his wife would handle the booking of all flights. Well, the film job didn't work out and he was back in two days.

We worked it out that I could take half the flights and he would provide a trike to fly. To say the trike was in very bad shape was a HUGE understatement. I completely rewired the wing and put on a new engine before doing any commercial flights. Gerry and I had totally different business and safety philosophies, so in very short order I decided to start my own operation.

There was more than enough business to support two trike tour operations on Kauai. The island had some of the busiest air space anywhere with seven helicopter operations at various locations on the island.

The first step for me was to get permission from the FAA Commercial Operations on Oahu to operate my business out of the Port Allen County Airport. The small airport kept quite busy with two helicopter tour operations, a sky diving business and Gerry's trike operation.

After submitting my flying credentials, completing a written letter of intention, and purchasing liability insurance from Lloyd's of London, I was given permission to operate a commercial flying business at Port Allen. I was assigned a location adjacent to Gerry's operation. This, of course, did not make him very happy -- but, as I have said, there was plenty of business for two operations.

I bought a new Air Creation Trike with a 912 four-stroke engine, flight suits, different size helmets to fit all heads, life jackets, and all the gear needed to offer quality flights to our customers. I finalized all my permits and licenses and started the tour operation called Kauai Ultralight Adventures. Tourists were always so excited to see the amazingly beautiful Kauai from the air, so we were busy right from the start.

All the gear was shipped to Kauai in a 24-foot enclosed trailer through Matson shipping lines. The shipment included all the gear as well as a new Dodge 4X4 truck with fuel tank in back.

I had to make each flight a training flight to comply with FAA regulations. To comply, I installed training bars on the glider and let everyone fly for a time from the back passenger seat. I gave each customer an introductory flight certificate. We hooked a Sony video disc recorder on the wing tip. It also recorded music I had playing from an IPod with a voiceover of our conversations and the flight towers.

I had the top 100 hits of each year, starting in 1966, downloaded on the IPod. I would ask each passenger what year they graduated from high school and then would play those hits to make it an even more memorable and personal flight. Customers could buy the video and audio recording of their flight experience and nearly every one of them did. We also had t-shirts with our logo available. We received a lot of residual business from those recordings because people always took them home and showed them to friends and family who, if they later traveled to Kauai, would book a flight with us.

I also had a list of all the schools on the mainland where customers could get flying lessons if they wanted to learn to fly trikes themselves.

Kauai, in my estimation, is the most beautiful island in the Hawaiian chain of islands. Waimea Canyon is much like Arizona's Grand Canyon. It is not as grandiose, but it is much more colorful with beautiful waterfalls, verdant landscapes, and vivid foliage. On one of the four flight options I offered, I took customers on flights up through the canyon near a beautiful waterfall and over the top at 5000-feet high. We would then go to a 4,000-foot drop through the Kalalau Valley with waterfalls cascading hundreds of feet to the clear blue waters of the Pacific.

The main flight pattern was along the Na Pali with beautiful beaches, sea caves and some of the most scenic cliffs in the world. A favorite experience was when we saw schools of spinner dolphins numbering 100 or more, huge green sea turtles smoothly swimming in the water and Monk Seals laying on the beaches. From December through mid-April, we experienced gigantic grey whales breaching out of the water, as well as mothers and babies gliding along the surface spouting as they went.

This open air flying experience had people gushing with commits like "that is the most incredible thing I have ever done." And believe me I completely understood as I felt so fortunate to be flying there and seeing these amazing sights myself.

Robert's first 912 Air Creation Clipper at Kauai Ultralight Adventures.

Once I got a call from a local elderly lady who wanted me to guarantee she would see whales if she bought a flight. I explained we couldn't guaranty a whale sighting, but at that time of year we saw them 90 percent of the time. She explained she was a volunteer whale counter, and it was the only reason she would go on the flight.

I offered 30-minute, 60-minute, 90-minute, and 2-hour around-the-entire-island flights. She finally booked an early morning 1-hour flight. She was excited and I flew right to the area where we usually viewed whales. On the way, while flying along the shoreline in front of the resorts, I spotted what looked like a whale in shallow water among the coral reefs. The thing that surprised me was that it wasn't moving, and this was unusual as they were normally in deeper water and swimming along. We flew on to the deeper water off the shore and sure enough a large whale breached right in front of us. We were flying low to the water, so it was a spectacular sighting. I always had a video camera running so I was able to capture it on video. She was "very happy" with her bird's eye view of whales.

She had purchased the shorter flight, so we turned around and retraced our flight route along the shore. When we got to the spot where I thought I had seen a whale, I spotted it again. The whale still was not moving so I did 180-degree turn and pointed it out to her. We did a complete circle so she could get a good view. Suddenly, a big cloud erupted from the whale and a baby whale was born right in front of our eyes! Yes, she was excited and so was I because I had never witnessed a birth before that trip. After we landed, the nice lady couldn't thank me enough. A few days later, a story about the experience appeared in the local Kauai newspaper.

Humpback Whales, Kauai.

There were many great whale experiences from the air, including spotting a whale that was stationary about mile off the west end of the airstrip. The whale was caught up in fishermen's netting and was hooked on the reef. I called the local Fish and Game Department, and they came out by boat with divers. Fortunately, they were successful and cut it free. It was a good feeling to know we spotted the whale in time for it to be freed and swim off to deeper water.

On another flight I saw a large tiger shark circling slowly around a full grown sea turtle. I knew sharks could bite open and eat smaller turtles because I had seen their broken shells on the NaPali beaches. But this turtle was really big. The shark looked to be at least a 10 to 12-footer. It made a sudden attack and started aggressively biting the turtle. They both churned the water surface until the turtle finally shook it off. I noticed strings of flesh streaming off it, possibly from the turtles under shell. I couldn't stay to watch as I had to get back for my next flight. To this day, I don't know if the shark was able to break open the full grown turtle. But it was quite a sight to experience first hard.

In my business, I also offered a flight out to the Island of Niihau which was 17.5 miles out over the sea to the West of Kauai. It included a flight around the island that took us over a quite large and shallow bay. We often saw whales and babies there. I was told that the whales liked the shallow waters for protection from tiger sharks.

Quite amazingly, Niihau is the only place in the world where people still speak Hawaiian as their primary language. The residents have their own dialect called Olelo Kanaka Niihau. I was fortunate to become good friends with one of the residents who worked as a night watchman at our airport. It was always interesting when his relatives came over to the airport on shopping errands. They would always speak in their Hawaiian tongue so I would stand close enough to listen to the dialect. The language is very nice and rather musical. It sounded a bit like Portuguese to me. The night watchman did invite me once to go visit Niihau with him, but unfortunately, I never made it.

I did take him on a flight there one afternoon. I hoped to land on the beach in front of their small village, but the sand looked too soft, so I opted not to chance getting stuck there. The island was a jewel to see from the air. It is now managed by two brothers, Bruce and Keith Robinson, who own the island with their family.

Islanders on Niihau are known for their gemlike shell leis made from Niihau shells. They are beautiful and quite expensive. The Robinson brothers now offer limited supervised hunting safaris of wild goats and wild boar. They fly their private helicopter to the island from the Port Allen field. They also have a hunting lodge located high on the side of Kauai above the airfield.

The island was dubbed the "Forbidden Isle" as it is off-limits to outsiders and only the Robinson family, their relatives, invited guests, government officials and U.S. Navy personal are allowed access. So, of course, I couldn't land anywhere on the island unless I was with the night watchman.

Views of a catamaran tour boat & spinner dolphins from the air, off Kauai.

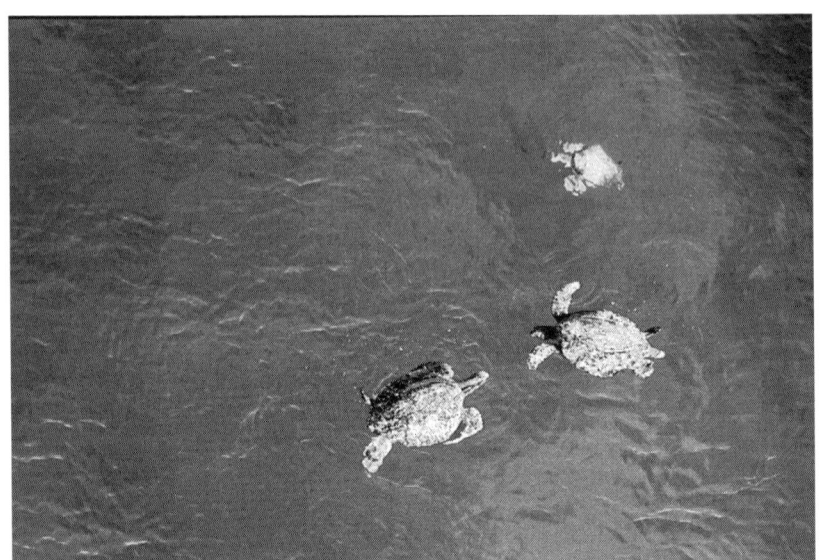

Flying above green sea turtles. The 4 previous photos are by Marius Jovaisa.

There was a great story written by one of my passengers during this time. The following is a reprint from the Seattle Post-Intelligencer October 12, 2006. It is an article written by author Herb Kavet in a "Special Hawaii Adventure Edition" about his experience flying with me at Kauai Ultralight Adventures. People loved the flight experience and Kavet wrote about his so eloquently. He has given me permission to reprint his words in this book.

Over Hawaii
Flying Over the Napali Coast
Tour Kauai quietly, gracefully like bird

There is no road traversing Kauai's awesome Na Pali Coast. To see it you must hike the rugged Kalalau Trail 11 miles each way or Kayak 17 miles of the sometimes-rough Pacific Ocean.

Helicopters can whisk you over the terrain, but it seems almost amoral to reach this dramatic beauty in such a noisy and mechanical manner. Not to mention getting stuck in the middle seat or having to contend with the kid in the back who throws up.

Catamaran and Zodiac tour boats let tourists see a part of the Na Pali, but the most breathtaking part.

The entire coast is a state park. Monumental 4000-foot cliffs plunge to crashing, foaming waves. Waterfalls cut cliffs like white ribbons falling hundreds of feet. The shore

114

is lined with volcanic sea caves and arches and beautiful sand beaches, some only accessible only by swimming. Verdant valleys, still showing signs of ancient terraced taro fields, separate the mountainous terrain.

This untamed coastline is one of the most scenic and least explored in the country. I decided the most exciting way to savor this special part of Kauai was to fly over it. But rather than go by light plane or helicopter, I wanted to experience it as the Wright brothers might have in a slow-moving open craft. I'd leave the closed in cabins and noisy engines of the helicopters for the "tourists"

A small company called Kauai Ultralight Adventures offers flights in an ultralight aircraft, nicknamed a trike, which it sort of resembles. It weighs less than 500 pounds, looks like a scooter with a fabric wing, can take off in as little as 50 feet and flies relatively quietly at a cruising speed of around 50 mph. The 10 gallon tank is good for about five hours of flying.

To fly several thousand feet above the earth in a tiny contraption lighter than most riding lawnmowers seemed a bit daunting at first. I've learned some common sense over the years, but I'm not cowed by heights. I was an Army paratrooper and just last year in Nepal I dove off a rickety bridge for what was billed as the world's highest bungee jump- something like 600 feet.

Still, the trike looked pretty flimsy.

A safety feature that convinced me to do it was the automatic emergency parachute. Should the wing crack in two or another emergency develop-whoosh! - a parachute would deploy just like an airbag in your car and we'd float gently to earth.

My $190 and I were ready to go up for an hour.

Though the weather was iffy, pilot Robert Combs agreed to give it a try. He outfitted me with helmet, goggles, floatation device, gloves, and flying suit. In sunny, warm Hawaii, that seemed superfluous, but it turned out it was a lot colder a few thousand feet above the ground.

I plunked down into sort of a lawn chair seat, my legs straddling the pilot in his own seat directly in front of me.
Conversation was easy using the built-in microphone and headset. The weather began clearing as he slowly taxied down a small runway, and before my heart could move into my throat, we were airborne.

This is how the birds must see Kauai - quiet, slow and graceful, soaring over scenic vantage points or dipping low to skim along the shore, with no anxiety.

We slowly gained altitude above Kauai's farmlands as smoke rose from fields where sugar cane was being burned.

The views as we reached the Na Pali Coast enveloped the senses with colors, depths and motion. Waterfalls plunged, precipices fell away, turtles stood out in the clear water and the sky engulfed us.

We peered from above into a cave whose roof was open. I had kayaked into the same cave a week before and bobbed rather nervously around the rubble of the ancient collapsed roof. This was totally different, soaring over it on air currents.

Robert let me take the controls for a while. Basically, you tilt the kitelike wing up or down or side to side. It was easy and I loved it, though I'll admit I was happy to turn it back to Robert when it came time to land.

Was an ultralight the best way to see the Na Pali Coast? It may beat hiking that rugged trail. I suspect that after hours of dazzling panoramas on foot, the mind shuts down and decides to concentrate on sore shoulder or blistered foot or numb fingers.

There may be some nervous moments on an ultralight, like when the pilot demonstrates its stability by taking his hands off the wing bars that steer the craft, but otherwise it is pure bliss.

When we flew over some catamaran cruise boats on our return to the tiny airstrip, we were greeted with wild waving and perhaps 50 cameras and videos recording our passing. It made me feel we were a special sight, maybe just a little like the magnificent coastline itself.

IF YOU GO *(based on rates in 2006 when this was written)*

~ $190 per hour, and one passenger per aircraft. However, the company has two ultralights, so a couple or two friends could fly at the same time and talk with their individual pilots and each other during flight via a radio/intercom system.

~ A video or still photos of each flight are available. Professional-grade cameras with wide angle lens are mounted to the wingtips of the aircraft for these shots. Or take your own with attached safety cords.

~ Flight suits and gloves are provided. Closed-toe shoes and socks are required (tennis shoes are OK). Long pants and a long-sleeved T-shirt or sweatshirt are best in winter months.

~ Flights take off from and return to Burns Field at Port Allen Airport in Hanapepe on the west side of the island.

Herb Kavet lives near Boston, and you can find his many great books on Amazon.

Kauai Ultralight Adventures.

Triking the NaPali coastline, Kauai, Hawaii.

Chapter 18
One of the Wettest Spots on Earth

Our two hour flights around the island took us to the one of the wettest spots on the earth, Mount Waialeale Crater. Waialeale means rippling or overflowing water. It is a 4000-foot wall face with 20 or more waterfalls pouring down its lush green face.

The Pacific trade winds bring in clouds around the 3000-foot level. These winds would collide with the crater wall and then be forced up and over the top. A lot of the cloud's moisture dropped down onto the wall face making it extremely lush and moist with many waterfalls. The flight into the crater wall face required plenty of speed with a high bank angle into, and then out of, the crater. It was a heart-pumping maneuver! I had to be sure there were no tour helicopters already in the crater before entering.

On the top of the crater, at 5,200 feet, is the Alaka'i Wilderness Preserve that has plant and insect life found nowhere else in the world. It also has many endangered endemic species that have been dramatically declining. Today, it is designated as a protected area.

I'm sure that when I flew there, it would overwhelm people a bit as I could hear them gasping through the headsets. I always had calming music playing in the headsets. You can probably imagine some of the comments people would make. But they loved it! And I loved sharing the area from our bird's eye prospective.

After about a year, I bought a second trike and hired another pilot so we could take couples or friends on flights at the same time. Prior to that, a second person had to hang out at the airport under the shade of our awning or at the beach at the end of the airstrip. We did provide a beach chair, umbrella, and cooler.

It was fun listening to them talk to each another on the flights. We had installed push-to-talk switches on their headsets, with microphones, so they could converse. Wow! Awesome! Spectacular! were some of the comments we heard time and time again.

About this time my son Chris, with his advanced computer knowledge (which I did not possess), created a great internet web page for our business. Well, I got to see the magic of the internet experience. In a short time, our business doubled. People were able to book the flights online before they even got to the island.

We had a memorable couple book flights through our web site. Unfortunately, one of the trikes was down for maintenance. So, the wife,

Peggy, decided to fly with me first. This was a little different as the wives usually wanted their husband to go first. They had both booked the two-hour Around the Island flights. While we took off, her husband headed for the beach to wait his turn.

After about an hour and a half into our flight, we were flying near the end of the spectacular Na Pali Coast, where I always let customers "fly" the trike from the back seat with training bars. I did this with Peggy. As she was flying, I continued to tell her about island highlights. One of the sites I always described was the large white globes that were NASA's satellite and spacecraft tracking station. As I was describing the tracking station, Peggy piped up and said, "I work for Nasa." I thought she meant she worked at the station on Kauai, so I said, "oh I have taken several of your coworkers flying." She said, "no I work at the Johnson Space Center in Houston." I casually said, "oh really, what do you do for them?" She chuckled and said, "I'm an astronaut!!!"

An astronaut in my trike?! ... *Holy Crap!!!*

Yes, I'm sure it took me a minute to reply. I casually responded, "OK, how am I doing Peggy?" She said, "you're doing just fine Robert." Of course, I let her fly the rest of the way to the airport.

I have read a lot about Peggy, whose full name is Sally Annette Whitson. She is an American biochemistry researcher and now is a retired NASA Astronaut and former NASA Chief Astronaut. She has a total of 665 days in space, more than any other woman or American.

Peggy sent me an autographed photo of her in her space suit thanking me for the flight. I also took her husband, Clarence for the two hour flight. He also worked for NASA and was a very interesting and nice guy to talk with along the flight. I have taken several celebrities flying over the years, but Peggy Whitson was by far the most interesting.

Peggy A. Whitson

Peggy sent me this autographed photo after her flight.
Flying with her was a once in a lifetime experience!

On another trip, one man booked the two-hour around the island flight. He showed up with a high end Nikon camera and lenses. I explained to him that we didn't allow passengers to take their cameras and lenses because, if they were to drop one, it would most likely go through our pusher prop causing us to go down. He told me he was Marius Jovaisa, a professional photographer from Lithuania and he only bought the flight to take photos. So, we worked out safety lines for his camera and he had a zipper bag, strapped around his waist, that he kept in his lap to hold the lenses. He promised he would be very careful and change the lenses while inside the bag. It was another beautiful day on Kauai, and he was leaning way out of the back seat shooting pictures like crazy. We saw dolphin, turtles, a monk seal on the beach and, of course, the canyon and the awesome Napali coastline.

Marius Jovaisa and Robert Combs.

I flew as close as I dared so he could get the best possible photos. When we got back to the airfield, he was very excited to see what he had captured. It was the last flight of the day, so we went into the trailer with his laptop along with my son Tim. We closed the door so it was dark, and Marius loaded the photos on his laptop so we could view them. Well, I was totally amazed with his photos! I had never seen the island in such splendor! Tim said, "wow dad, those are the best pictures I've ever seen." I completely agreed.

After thinking about it, I asked Marius if he was interested in making an aerial photo book of Kauai. I said, "I'll provide all the flights and you take the pictures." He said he had already made a book from the air of his home country of Lithuania, and he had everything already lined up for printing and publishing. He agreed and we set to work flying over Kauai and Niihau for the next two weeks. We flew in the early mornings and late evenings because he said it was the best light for memorable photographs.

We decided we wanted to get a photo of Kauai in its entirety with the sun coming up out of the ocean on the horizon. This required taking off in the dark, flying out to sea with a climb to more than 12,000 feet. Marius was unable to wear the usual flight helmet with visor because he couldn't get his camera to his eye with it on, so he borrowed my prized Mount Cook ski hat. Shortly after takeoff, there was a sudden WHOMP sound, and the engine stalled for a second. It really gave me quite a scare and I asked Marius "what was that"? The hat had blown off his head and went through the prop. You must remember; we were out in the middle of the ocean, in the dark, and it took a couple of minutes to check out the engine gauges. Miraculously, all was OK, and we got to altitude just before the sun rose on the ocean horizon. The sun lit up the entire Island of Kauai. Marius got a spectacular shot and to this day, it is still one of my favorites.

Marius completed the book of aerial photographs of Hawaii. It turned out great. I also sold some of the best photos, that were enlarged in frame quality formats, in our Water Glide store in Hanapepe. Marius and I worked on another book years later in Belize, which I talk about later in this book. The Belize book is currently in its second printing.

The flight along the Napali coast required flying through the controlled airspace of the U.S. Military Missile Base on the North end of Kauai. Almost daily, I had to make a radio call to their flight operations tower for their permission to fly through their controlled air space. Over time, I got quite used to speaking to the controllers.

One day, while on a two hour flight with a customer, I approached the home airport of Port Allen and there was a weather system with heavy rain over the airfield. I decided to turn around and fly back to a small airstrip along the beach and land there to wait for the weather to pass. But, when I arrived at the airstrip, the weather system was approaching too fast to make a safe landing. My only other option was the Missile Base because I was low on fuel.

I called the tower and asked if I could make an emergency landing as civilian aircraft were not usually allowed to land at the base. The tower operator gave me permission and asked me to report my distance altitude and heading as I approached. I did and landed near the tower as he directed.

What happened next was quite memorable. As soon as we touched down, a P2 fire truck with all the red lights flashing, and a white car with its lights flashing, drove up to us. The tower operator told me to follow the car. It led us to one of the giant hangars. Soon, the door opened, and we taxied in next to several military F15 fighter jets and two huge C-5 Galaxy cargo jets. The trike looked like a miniature toy next to them. I jumped out and started to take a cell phone photo of the scene. The officer quickly walked up to me and sternly said "no photos. I got the message and said, "yes sir."

He introduced himself as the base commander. We got into his car, and he drove us through the wind and rain to the tower. He took us to the top control room of the tower and introduced us to the controller. We watched the weather system come and move out quickly which is rather typical on the islands. My passenger called his wife who was waiting at Port Allen and told her what happened. She was relieved to hear we were safe.

It was great to meet and talk in person to one of the military air traffic controllers that I had been talking to on almost a daily basis. Once the weather passed, the base commander took us back to the trike. We shook hands, I thanked him, he said we were the first civilian aircraft to land at the base. It was a great experience and reminded me of my military days in the U.S. Air Force. We loaded up and flew in calm weather back to Port Allen.

Another interesting customer at that time was a Hawaiian fisherman. He was a big Samoan man who weighed close to 300 pounds. He owned two boats that were used to net schools of Mackerel. Since he was a true Hawaiian, it was legal for him to net large schools of fish. I gave him a handheld aviation radio that he gave to one of his boat captains. The plan was to go to an area along the shoreline where there were usually large schools of fish. The mackerel looked like large dark clouds in the water and the shape from the air looked like a hurricane with an eye in the middle.

I gave him a headset with a push-to-talk button so he could talk directly to the boat captain. We circled around 150 to 200 feet above the boat, and he directed them to the desired location. They would then throw the large net, towed by the boat, and encircle the school of fish with the net. It really worked well, and they would come away with a large catch most every time. We became good friends, and he would invite me to his home for holiday family celebrations like Christmas. These gatherings were always so much fun with plenty of fantastic home cooked Hawaiian food. And yes, you guessed it, plenty of fresh caught local fish.

124

As our flying business grew, I rented a building next to the main road leading to Waimea Canyon. It was in the small village of Ele'ele near our airport. There were two buildings on the property. One was set more to the rear and the other bordered the road. I used the rear building as a shop for trike maintenance. We converted the other building into a store where we sold all kinds of kites, mounted photos of the island that we had taken from the aircraft, t-shirts with our logo, and sunglasses, etc. We also used the location to sell flights when we had openings.

A highlight of the operation was a wall-mounted large screen TV that had a loop running featuring footage from our trike flights. My son Chris, who was then 18, ran the store and lived in the apartment above it. He enjoyed living on his own and did a great job running the store. My younger son Timothy, was 16 and then became my ground crew and was responsible for fueling the aircraft between flights, putting flight suits and CO_2 fired life jackets on the customers and getting them to sign the liability release forms.

Timothy loved flying with me in the trike. Both boys had been flying with me in hang gliders and ultralights since they were 5 years old. Christopher went to Arizona on the "Mainland" as we Hawaiians called it and learned to fly trikes on his own with my long time pilot friend John Beeman. John said Chris was a "natural".

John was an instructor for John Kemmeries who owned Air Creation USA FBO Flight School. After Chris got his rating, he took his younger brother on an around the Kauai Island two hour flight. I am quite proud of my two boys.

I got my first Ultralight rating and flight instructor rating from John in Peoria, Arizona. Ole Olson, a long time hang glider pilot friend of mine, also worked there as an instructor.

I also flew with Ole at the Sky Gypsy Complex owned by John McAfee (of McAfee Antivirius software business) in Rodeo, N.M. Ole has written three books about his adventures flying hang gliders and trikes in the USA and Mexico. They are titled, *Tales From the Wild Blue Yonder, *Taking Mexico Flying*; Tales From the Wild Blue Yonder, *Living Dangerously Olson, John Q*; and Tales From the Wild Blue Yonder, *Recipes for Disaster*.*

I highly recommend them. They are a great read and can be purchased on Amazon.

Chris Combs proudly poses with trike during flight school.

Timothy, Robert, passenger, and Chris on Kauai.

Chapter 19
More Training and a New Adventure

At the end of 2007, the FAA took over governing control of ultralight flying in the United States. I flew to Los Angeles and began flight school to get my Sport Pilot License. I passed the FAA written and practical flight tests and then flew to McAfee's Sky Gypsy complex to work on my instructor's certification.

Soon after this, McAfee asked me to go to Belize with him to start a light sport flight operation like the one I had in Hawaii. Being the adventurer, I was ready for a new experience.

I returned to Kauai to discover that one of my aircraft (with very low hours) took a direct hit by a waterspout. A waterspout is like a tornado on land, but on land it can do a lot of damage. This one came off the sea, made a direct hit and totaled my trike that was covered and securely tied down to my enclosed trailer on the field. At this point I had been flying flight tours on Kauai for more than five years. I decided to take McAfee up on his offer to start a business in Belize.

John bought a beautiful place right on the beach of Ambergris Caye. It was on the north end of the island above the village of San Pedro. Amazingly, the small village had its own airstrip that ran parallel with the lay of the narrow island.

The prevailing winds in the area come out of the north. All the air traffic which was mostly Cessna Caravans with turbo prob engines carrying tourists to and from San Pedro. Surprisingly, they were required to take off downwind to the south, so they did not overfly the village after takeoff. This was not a real problem for them as the planes were so powerful. Even with a full load of 14 passengers and cargo, I watched them take off in a 15 MPH tailwind.

It worked for the Cessnas, but it was not possible for me to operate a trike tour business in these conditions. Even with the 100 HP 912S engine on the French Air Creation Tanarg Aircraft which John had already shipped to San Pedro, it was not a safe possibility. Plus, the wind was a daily occurrence. I figured there was only enough time to get one flight in during the early morning before the winds started blowing. John had also purchased a hangar on the airstrip. To say the least, he was disappointed to learn this. I told him it would only be a matter of time before there would be a stall and crash when taking off in a downwind with the trike.

However, there was another location just South of Ambergris called Caye Caulker that had an airstrip. Fortunately, this one was laid out in such a way that you could take off into the prevailing wind. I told John about it, and he asked me to look for a lot to buy next to the field. His idea was to build a hangar and set up an operation. I found a nice lot for sale in a good location right next to the airfield and he decided to buy it. However, greed stepped in. When the owners heard that it was the very wealthy John McAfee who would buy the land., they more than doubled their price. Of course, this angered John immensely and he backed out.

While on Caye Caulker, I met a trike pilot from Canada named Walter Martin. Walter had recently purchased a float trike, but had no time on floats. I did, so I taught him to fly his float trike over a two week time period. Walter was a great guy and a good student. He and his wife, a pro scuba diving instructor, owned a real nice townhouse on Caye Caulker.

So, at this point I had had enough and traveled up to the north end of Belize on the border of Guatemala to the Cayo District. There is a village there called San Ignacio. I had heard there was a guy named Mike who was flying an ultralight near a Jungle Lodge called Chaa Creek. I decided to try and find him.

I found Mike, who was flying a small single place trike with a Rotax 503 engine, working for Mick Fleming who owned the Lodge along with his wife Lucy. Lucy was from the United States and Mick was from England. The Lodge, located in the jungle along the Macal River, was amazing. It has beautifully decorated cottages with palm thatch roofs tying into the rustic, tropical beauty of the area.

Mick and Lucy moved there in 1977 and began growing the resort from one extra cottage (for their friends who came to visit) to the Eco Lodge that it is today. Chaa Creek has a restaurant and bar, beautiful large swimming pool, horseback riding and canoeing on the river. Mick has quite a green thumb and grows a variety of vegetables in his wonderous garden. These vegetables are prepared and served in their restaurant. He even grows pitahaya fruit (also known as dragon fruit) that makes the most delicious ice cream. They employ more than 100 local people from a nearby village. Several members of the staff have been working for Mick & Lucy for more than 20 years.

Well, it turned out that Mick wanted to learn to fly a light sport trike and it was perfect timing for me in Belize. His neighbor owned a large cornfield and Mick talked with him about the possibility of designing and building a grass airstrip. Mick introduced me to Amen Bedran, his neighbor, and we came up with a plan for me to design and oversee the airstrip construction. A great benefit of the job was that it included a cabin next to the airfield where I could stay while building the airstrip.

The airstrip was specifically designed to be long enough for Cessna Caravans also to land. This worked out great for Mick's resort and other resorts nearby as their guests could now fly from the main airport in Belize City to the resorts. Our airstrip was so popular that we had a couple fly ins with planes coming from all over Belize. The airstrip was later paved and is now very busy with commercial operations.

Mick asked me to help him pick out and buy a new ultralight trike. I recommend an Australian Airborne Outback trike that would be perfect to learn on and it would be a good intermediate glider for him as well. I knew the guys at Airborne, and they built a quality light sport aircraft which is what the planes were known as after the FAA took over the governing of the sport. I ordered a 912S Outback for Mick and arranged for my second AirCreation 912S Clipper to be shipped to Belize.

We started building a hangar to house all the aircraft. About this time, Amin asked me what I would recommend for a premium light sport aircraft. I told him, if money was no object, I would buy an AirCam. It was a tandem two-place with twin Rotax 912S engines, open cockpit and fixed wing that was built by Phil Lockwood of Lockwood Aircraft in Florida. At that time, the amateur built kit was priced around $100,000 and another $40,000 to have it professionally built. And it usually took four or five months to build. He asked me if we could find a good used one. I told him the best option to find a used one was in Southern Florida.

Amin started pursuing it and making calls to locate one. I also started researching options and found one for sale near Orlando. The guy said it had low hours and he wanted $80,000 for it. Amin asked me to go to Florida and check it out. The aircraft was in very good condition because the owner kept it in a hangar. Amin said to buy it. I recommended we take it to Lockwood and have them check it out first. He agreed, so the owner flew it to Lockwood Aircraft.

I had never met Phil, but I had ordered a new Rotax engine from his company while in Hawaii. He had designed and built the single engine Drifter. Later, he was hired to do some filming work in Africa and knew he would be flying over miles of dense jungle, so he designed the twin engine AirCam to provide added safety. The AirCam could fly on just one engine. In fact, it could climb at 500 feet per minute on just one of its 912S 100 HP Rotax engines. It became so popular that as of 2019, he had sold more than 250 twin engine AirCam kits.

129

In looking back, I liked him right away because he was smart, and his operation was first class. He gave me a thumbs up on the AirCam. I asked him if I could make a three-place craft out of it by adding a third seat. I thought an additional seat and headsets could be installed directly behind the second seat in the luggage compartment. He said his shop couldn't do the work, but he would sell me the parts and let me build it in his shop. That was great.

Phil put me in touch with a friend that built AirCam kits for customers. He was super professional and greatly helped me with the project. We also installed an auxiliary 24-gallon fuel tank with an electric fuel pump. It pumped the fuel directly into one of the fuel tanks in the wing. We then installed a crossover fuel line between the two tanks in the wings to allow fuel to be transferred equally between the tanks. This also made the fuel gauge for each tank read correctly, including the fuel from the auxiliary tank.

We did all these modifications needed so we could fly the AirCam from Orlando to Key West and then across the Gulf of Mexico to the coastline of Cuba. My flight plan was to land in Cuba, but the air traffic controllers required us to stay 12 miles off their coast, so we flew on to Cancun, Mexico. From there we charted a plan from Cancun along the coast of the Yucatan Peninsula, and then to Belize. The final leg was on to our airstrip.

I didn't have twin engine time, so Phil set up lessons with one of his friends who owned an AirCam on amphibious floats. We planned on adding amphibious floats on ours once we had it in Belize, so this was ideal. I had quite a bit of float time already and sea ratings in my logbook as I had owned an amphib ultralight trike in Lake Havasu.

Amin had a future brother-n-law who was a commercial cargo pilot and asked me if he could go along for the trip. I agreed and we set off on our adventure.

Robert flying the AirCam in Belize.

We waited for a high pressure system to set up in Key West and then took off across the Gulf. Since the controller in Cuba wouldn't let us fly in their airspace, this kept us out of sight of the Island. We checked our fuel burn at the halfway point and had more than half of our fuel left and a very light headwind, so we continued on. At one point we came across a cruise ship, so we flew down low close and circled it. We could see passengers waving at us. They must have thought we were quite a sight with our open cockpit and our luggage stacked high on top of the extra fuel tank and third seat. Especially since we were way out in the middle of the ocean!

Later that day, we landed in Cancun and still had 10 gallons of fuel left. We had been in the air just over six hours. After clearing customs, we overnighted there and set off for Belize early the next morning. It was a spectacular flight along the shoreline of the Yucatan, Mexico. We took turns at the flight controls and flew low over the beaches and the many beachfront resorts along the Yucatan Peninsula.

Later, we crossed over the border into Belize and the sea took on that beautiful Caribbean blue hue. I called John McAfee on Ambergris Caye and he came out on his dock and gave us a wave. We circled low to the water by him and then continued to Belize City Airport.

131

After landing, the Belizean customs agents met us at the airport tarmac. What took us only five minutes to clear customs in Cancun, took us four hours in Belize. They made us unload all our luggage so they could open our bags and search everything. The paperwork part dragged on and on. We were glad to finely get cleared, so we called our friends at Chaa Creek and said we were on our final leg to the new airstrip.

We decided to call the airstrip "Maya Flats" and had it written out on top of the two hangars. It turned out very nice with the thick grass that we had planted. I could easily see the bright orange windsock from my cabin, so I always knew if the wind conditions were good for flying.

A great aerial view of the Maya Flats hangers.

Chapter 20
Writing the Rules and World Record Flights

In 2008, Manuel Heredia Jr., the Minister of Tourism and Civil Aviation in Belize, and Jose A. Contreras, the Civil Aviation Director, appointed me President of the newly formed Light Sport Aviation Association in Belize.

This job required a lot of diverse knowledge, including the writing of rules governing all flight of Light Sport Aircraft. I copied most of the rules set down by the US FAA, except the rule governing the AirCam. I made the AirCam an Advanced Light Sport Aircraft which was extremely important for our plans because the new rules allowed it to be used commercially as a three-place aircraft. In this way we could legally take couples for flight tours in Belize.

A couple of months after the appointment, Mr. Heredia showed up with a large bag of confetti. He asked me if I would fly over his village with the AirCam and dump the confetti during the Belize Independence Day Celebration parade. I agreed and it was a hit. Everybody loved the show, and I made points with the Minister.

About this time, I wrote to Marius Jovaisa in Lithuania and told him I had moved to Belize. I invited him to visit and see if he would be interested in shooting aerial photos for a book of Belize. Marius ended up visiting several times and stayed for nearly two weeks each time. I had arranged accommodations for he and I at four different resorts, including one on a Caye out on the picturesque reef.

Two of the resorts we photographed were owned by Francis Ford Coppola -- the Turtle Inn on the beach of the Placencia Peninsula and the Blancaneaux Lodge located in the Mountain Pine Ridge Reserve. The Turtle Inn ended up on the cover of our book, "Heavenly Belize".

We spent many mornings and evenings in the air covering the entirety of Belize. We named the book "Heavenly Belize". The first edition had an introduction written by the Honorable Manuel Heredia Jr., Belize Minister of Tourism, Culture and Civil Aviation. It was a great success. The second printing's introduction was written by the Honorable Dean Barrow, Prime Minister of Belize.

Not too long after, I met a German pilot flying a float trike. His name was Andreas Zmuda and he was flying out of a small airport near San Ignacio in Belize. Andreas told me of his plan to buy a new trike and fly it around the world. His idea was similar to trike pilots, Olivier Aubert and Mike Blyth, who in 1999 flew for 27,000 miles during their eight month flying adventure that goes beyond the imagination. Olivier and Mike shipped their trikes to Buenos Aires, Argentina. They then flew them to Santiago, Chili, and then up the west coast of South and Central America, and then along the east coast of the United States and Canada. From there they crossed the North Atlantic and flew through Greenland, along Iceland and then down through Europe into Africa. From there, they flew through the whole of Africa to its Southern tip.

They made a film about their flying adventure named "South to South" It's one of my all-time favorite flying films of trike flying. Their flight is known as the Millennium Microlight Adventure, and it was dubbed the "last great flying adventure" of the 20th century.

Well, Andreas did achieve his goal. At the time of this writing, he and his girlfriend Doreen Kroeber have flown their trike through 56 countries around the world. You can follow them and their trike flying adventures by looking on the internet or Facebook under Trike Globetrotter Project. When they began their adventure, they stopped in Belize, and we had a Bon Voyage party for them. That was over 10 years ago, and they are still going! They also have videos of their flying adventures you can purchase online.

In 2014 and 2015, Andreas and Doreen spent 13 months traveling around the world in their trike. They visited 35 countries and five continents for an amazing 87,314 miles.

Andreas Zmuda & Doreen Krober.

Cayes of Belize.

Chapter 21
More Adventures in Belize

I was hired by a realtor to fly him over the largest living reef in the Western Hemisphere to view and photograph some of The Cayes that he was listing for sale. These Cayes, as they are called, are hundreds of small islands in this region which has made it a popular destination for people wanting almost total privacy. Ringo Star and Leonardo DiCaprio were a couple of the famous owners of these islands. Being able to see the islands from the bird's eye perspective of the trike helped make the selling experience easier.

After completing that job, he referred me to another client who he had sold a Caye to, who was planning to build a resort on his scenic Caye. His client was living in London. The realtor said his client was looking for someone to manage the building of a resort and that I should apply for the job.

He was kind enough to set up a time for my interview. I flew my trike to the small village of Placencia on the southern end of Belize. And as luck would have it, the village had a small airstrip. From there, I was picked up by boat for a 19 mile trip out to a beautiful Caye that was known, at that time, as Hatchet Caye. It later became known as Ray Cay when purchased by another owner. During the interview I was asked about my past employment which was all self- employed in Hawaii, Florida, North Carolina, Arizona, and Belize. Legally, according to the FAA, we were not supposed to call our flying "tour operations", but that is essentially what they were.

I told him that I always let passengers take a turn at flying the trikes with instructions on the basic controls. They were straight forward on how they flew. You had to push out on the control bar to climb with power, pull in on the control bar to go down without power. If you wanted to make a right turn, pull your right elbow to your right side while holding the control bar and looking to the right and so carving a nice turn. And the opposite for a left turn. It felt very much like you had wings growing out of your back, flying like a bird. It really was a very fun feeling!

When the owner found out I was a light sport pilot and instructor, he asked if I could help him purchase two trikes with floats so they could fly them from the resort. He also asked if I could teach him to fly them. I told him that I would provide instructions on flying them off wheels first and that we could do it at our Maya Flats Airstrip in San Ignacio, Belize. He said "OK. Here's a credit card. Let's order them!"

I thought about it for a minute and then said, "I guess that means I'm hired to manage the building of your resort". We discussed my wage, and he was very generous. I told him of a friend of mine, now living in London, that could help with the bookkeeping aspect of the job. He said I could hire her. I called my friend and offered her the job with very good pay, and she was looking forward to the adventure of living and working on a beautiful Caribbean Island.

Shortly thereafter, I called Scott Johnson in Idaho who was the dealer for Airborne Australia and ordered two Airborne Outback trikes with 912S 100 HP engines and floats. We added a nice size hangar to the building plans and looked forward to seeing what would transform on the island.

The resort buildings were being built in Los Angles. After constructing, they would be disassembled and shipped to Belize for the reconstruction process.

I had to keep enough food on hand to feed 27 construction workers. We had a large barge built to get all the building materials and heavy equipment out to the island. We also constructed a state-of-the-art solar system to power the entire resort and a freshwater swimming pool next to the restaurant and bar. Several cottages were constructed along the shore with stunning views of the Caribbean waters.

During the process, we dredged up enough sand to add two acres to the existing five acres of island. We also built three large dock systems to access the grounds. It was a huge project that took two years to complete.

It turned out to be a beautiful resort. They had several boats -- one boat just for fishing, another for diving operations and one to shuttle visitors the 19 miles across the water from Placencia Village out to the resort. They had kayaks, Hobie Cat sailing boats, wind surfing and of course diving and snorkeling on the largest natural reef in the Western Hemisphere.

Once my job of overseeing the construction phase was finished, the owner hired a regular resort manager and staff to run it. The resort is still in operation today and is called Ray Caye Island Resort.

I taught the owner to fly his trikes on our grass strip at Maya Flats. The floats arrived sometime later, and the dealer had hired a man from Florida to come down to Belize and build the amphib's on the trikes. Unfortunately, he didn't have all the parts needed to complete the job, so he left and never returned. I tried to get the parts and finish it myself, but never could. It was really a shame because the floats themselves were quality.

After I left Belize, the owner hired a trike pilot from Perth, Australia, to attach the floats (without the gear wheels) to one of the trikes. I later saw an aerial photo of that pilot flying it around the island. I was glad to see it operational.

By this time, I had been in Belize nearly four years and was now ready to head back to my home state of Montana.

When the financial bank crash of 2008 hit tourism fell off completely and Mick had to temporarily close his resort. He kept his employees, which numbered over 100, working enough to survive, but it was hard times. Thankfully, due to good planning and resourcefulness, he was able to open the resort again. It is a hugely popular destination to this day.

Flying over a Caye Resort in Belize.

Chapter 22
Who Me? Go on a Dating Site. No Way!

Before leaving Belize, my friend Mick Fleming, who owns Chaa Creek Jungle Resort, and I were sitting in his hangar after a day of trike flying over beautiful jungles and rivers. We were relaxing in lounge chairs in the open hangar door and discussing life. I was 65 then and Mick asked what I was going to do with the rest of my life? He said you are not getting any younger and he wanted to know if I was going to continue being a nomad or would I finally settle down.

Mick said, "You wouldn't believe how many couples at the resort tell me they met on an internet dating site." I said I couldn't imagine how you could tell if you were compatible with a person from photos and letters.

It got me thinking and as fate would have it, I decided to try it. I investigated a senior dating site and it required that you include your zip code when writing your bio. They did this so you could meet people in your area. Knowing I would be going to Montana, I put in the Flathead Valley zip code.

I did it, but still thought nothing would come out of it. I would be WRONG.

One person caught my attention right away. She was a pretty woman named Darlene who had an interesting story. She had been a newspaper writer and editor, then Vice President of Marketing for a very large banking and investment firm, before opening her own large advertising agency in Florida. Over the years, she published many books, and one received an international award of excellence. In 2003, she sold her company and returned to her home state of Montana.

I started writing to her and said I was working in Belize, but would be coming back to Montana that summer. We wrote back and forth for a month when she asked what I liked to do for fun. I mentioned my love of hang gliding. She said, "Oh, I have flown a hang glider." I said, "really ... where?" She said in Montana. I immediately responded "really, with who?". With so many years of flying in Montana, I figured I would know any pilots from there. She said, "Ed Burris."

I thought to myself, I know her! After a minute or so, I wrote back and said, "OH! You are THAT Darlene!"

You see I had a different girlfriend back then and we used to go on hang gliding adventures and have hang gliding meetings at Moose's Saloon in Kalispell. Darlene was a news editor for The Daily Interlake Newspaper.

At one time, she wrote a story and took photos about a hang gliding meet in around 1977. I remembered her very well as she was smart and quite good looking with long dark hair and striking blue eyes. Well, as fate would have it, I HAD to meet her again.

To this day, I marvel at how we connected on a dating site, even though we were living thousands of miles apart. I was in a warm jungle paradise, and she was in the frigid, yet picturesque mountains. I returned to Montana that summer and we saw each other for the first time in 40 years on July 4th, 2013, in Whitefish. We have been together ever since.

Robert and Darlene at their favorite waterfall in Glacier Park.

I took my girl Darlene to the Sun & Fun Airshow in Lakeland, Florida, a few years back. She loved getting to see all the different light sport aircraft, including an Easy Riser, and one of Larry Newman's Ultralight Eagles. I owned both in my early flying days.

But what she enjoyed the most was a tandem hang gliding flight she went on with Malcolm Jones at Wallaby Ranch near Orlando. I towed up right behind them and after releasing from our tow planes, we got to fly close by each other. Malcom had a video camera mounted, and captured a shot of us flying together. After that memorable flight, I started calling her my "Lady Hawk".

Lady Hawk's maiden flight. Robert is flying just below to the right.

A year or so later, we were living in Bigfork on the North end of Flathead Lake. While out one day, I met Todd Ware who had a trike flying operation geared toward injured military personnel. His flight school was called Air Therapy Aviation and he enjoyed taking people flying in the Flathead.

About that time, I became partners in a trike which gave me the ability to freely fly around the Flathead Valley. I also flew again in Lake Havasu during the winter months.

About a year later, I met Matt Johnson at the Ferndale Airport near Bigfork. Matt and his wife, Lisa, moved to the area from back East. Matt was also a pioneer hang glider pilot out East and flew with early pilot, Dennis Pagan. Dennis wrote several books on hang gliding, and I met him at flying competitions over the years.

Matt also owns and flies light sport trikes. He spent nearly two years building a four-place amphibian aircraft called the Seawind. He had it professionally painted by Jim Straube who also lived on Kauai for many years, but now lives in the mountains near Condon, MT. It is a beautiful airplane and Matt showed it at the Oshkosh Air Show in Wisconsin during the summer of 2023. More than 700,000 people attended that show and his Seawind was a big hit with thousands of people stopping to see it and ask questions.

I have been fortunate to go to the Oshkosh Air Show with Matt several times over the years. He is an amazing friend, pilot, and designer.

I also met George Tuma at the Ferndale Airport. George took me on amazing soaring flights in in his Stemme Motor Glider. The Stemme is a two-place sailplane with a 75- foot wingspan and Rotax turbo charged engine. It has a propeller in the nose that folds out when under power and back into the nose when shut off.

Above is George's Stemme at the Ferndale Airport.

On one of our flights, we flew with the motor off for nearly two hours on just a glide in marginal ridge lift. We actually had to deploy the dive brakes a couple times to stay out of the clouds. The dive brakes are a mechanical gadget that pops up out of the wings and interrupts the lift produced by the wing. The Stemme gets about a 50-to-1 glide. That means it can glide forward 50 feet for every foot of sink. Our best hang gliders get about 20 to 1.

These photos are of Matt Johnson's Seawind at the Oshkosh Air Show in Wisconsin, 2023. It was a week filled with incredible aviation sights and memorable experiences.

In these retirement years, I have also met Henry Imagawa who is a trike pilot turned gyro pilot from Southern California. He comes to Montana to fly with us each summer. Henry is a master videographer and has made many spectacular videos of his flights around the Western U.S. He shows these flights on his YouTube channel under Henry Trikelife and Henry GyroLife.

One of my most spectacular trike flights was with Henry when we flew our trikes up and over Glacier National Park. Henry videoed these flights and added nice music to them. Check it out and others on his YouTube channel.

A spectacular view of Glacier National Park, Montana.

Chapter 23
Flying in My 70s!

OK, I know I was 30 only about 10 years ago which would make me 40 -- right? But my driver's license says I'm in my mid-70s at the writing of this book. How in the world did that happen so fast? I was living life to the fullest. I thought growing old would take longer.

During the last several years, I was able to get a couple amazing hang gliding flights high above the Swan Mountain Range. Flying this range is spectacular because once you have worked your way up in thermals, you can find yourself a couple thousand feet above the top of the range. It takes my breath away every time I fly there. You're able to look back into the peaks of Glacier National Park and to the remote areas around the Hungry Horse Reservoir and Bob Marshall Wilderness.

But the years have caught up and I have not one, but two, major shoulder surgeries as well as a scary surgery on my lower spine. "Gee, I wonder what caused those injuries? Oh, yes, I remember, we did have a few rough landings while learning to fly and there was that big crash in Hawaii."

After my second shoulder surgery I sold my hang gliding equipment to Justin Woods. Justin is a fireman in Whitefish, MT. Justin and his wife, Lexi, also own and operate Wild River Adventures, a river rafting company in West Glacier. Lexi is an officer in the U.S. Air Force Reserves. They have two children and are the busiest people I know. They have built a beautiful log home on their property in West Glacier. Justin has made me proud of his ability to fly hang gliders and is now pursuing paragliding and general aviation. He is also an amazing ice and mountain climber.

Lexi met her husband, Justin, through my daughter Jessica while they served in the Air Force together. Jessica is a Lieutenant Colonel in the Air Force and works for the Pentagon. She is married to Colby Lenz and they have four children, including my granddaughter, Madison. Colby is a retired Navy officer and now is a commercial airline pilot. All their kids are into high school sports and doing well keeping their parents very busy.

We also have "friends of a feather" Brian Johnson and his incredibly special and beautiful wife Bev. Brian and I spent many hours flying the spectacular mountain sites around the Flathead's Swan Mountain Range and Glacier National Park in the late 1970s. Of course, we flew our beloved Teakettle Mountain at the edge of Glacier Park. Brian, Bev, Darlene and I have become great friends.

Brian and Bev Johnson prepare for a tandem flight off Teakettle Mountain in the '70s. Kirk Burris holds the glider nose wires.

Brian and I have both retired from hang gliding now. We were born a month apart at the hospital in Whitefish in 1947. That makes us 76 years old at the time of this writing. Brian and Bev enjoy touring on their beautiful Harley "Screaming Eagle" and visiting new places on their electric bikes. They still explore the waters of Montana in their kayaks and enjoy camping whenever they can.

Darlene and I travel whenever we can, and we also enjoy riding our electric bikes around Montana and up in Glacier Park. We love everything about beautiful Flathead Lake.

My head tells me I can still do it all, but my body tells me a totally different story.

Debbie and Kirk Burris are ready to fly tandem in the '70s.

Ed Burris's son, Kirk, who I have flown gliders with for many years, and his wife, Debbie, are still friends after nearly 50 years. They enjoy snowmobiling and operating a great boat tour business on Flathead Lake. They also enjoy fun getaways to warmer weather in the winter months.

In closing, I will always feel fortunate to have been born in the time that allowed me to experience the joys of free flight through hang gliding. Yes, indeed, I have been lucky to enjoy "The Wings of Men" because we flew just like the soaring birds!

As Leonardo da Vinci said ...

"When once you have tasted flight, you will forever

walk the earth with your eyes turned skyward,

for there you have been, and there you long to return. "

It has been such a wonderful gift!

Made in the USA
Middletown, DE
10 July 2024

57059196R00084